LIVING
THE HERO'S
JOURNEY

LIVING THE HERO'S JOURNEY

EXPLORING YOUR ROLE IN THE ACTION-ADVENTURE OF A LIFETIME

WILL CRAIG

"An indispensable map of self-discovery for navigating the road less traveled and discovering the hero within."
~ **Jack Canfield**, Co-Author of *The Success Principles™* and *Chicken Soup for the Soul®*

"Every now and then a book comes along that takes you places you've never been before. *Living the Hero's Journey* is one of those books!"
~ **Marshall Goldsmith,** Author of #1 *New York Times* bestseller – *Triggers*

"Will Craig guides you on an exciting inner journey where you discover the hero in you. It's like an expedition to a mysterious new world with your own personal adventure guide. Become the star of your own movie!"
~ **Chérie Carter-Scott, Ph.D. MCC**, Mother of Coaching and #1 *NYT* bestselling author of *If Life is a Game, These are the Rules*

"If you want a rich, exciting, and adventure-filled life, read this book and become the hero of a life well lived."
~ **Mark Victor Hansen,** Co-Author of *Chicken Soup for the Soul®*

"Not since Joe Campbell has there been such a rich opportunity to cast yourself in the epic role you deserve in life and work!"
~ **Mark C. Thompson**, *NYT* bestselling author and World's #1 Executive Coach

"*Living the Hero's Journey* offers a fresh and fun approach to discovering your true path. It's entertaining, it's intelligent, and it's transformational."
~ **Marci Shimoff,** #1 *NYT* bestselling author, *Happy for No Reason* and *Chicken Soup for the Woman's Soul*

"Crafted with profound purpose and application. I've been immersed since I turned the first page. Watching the journey unfold, it is fascinating to see and feel myself as the character in the role of a lifetime."
~ **Lynn Price,** Social Entrepreneur (Oprah's Angel Network)

"Seldom is there a book that so decisively affects change in one's life. *Living the Hero's Journey* provides practical insights into knowing ourselves and loving what we discover."
~ **Judith E. Glaser**, Author of #1 bestseller–*Conversational Intelligence*

"Curious about your purpose and significance? *Living the Hero's Journey* is the guide you need to discover the life you were meant to live. Engaging, fun, and filled with rich examples."
~ **Marcia Reynolds, PsyD**, **MCC**, Author of *The Discomfort Zone* and Past Global President of the International Coach Federation

"This book is like having a good friend who's not afraid to tell it like it is—all the while offering hope, clear direction, and heartfelt guidance along the way. Where do you find that these days?"
~ **Greg S. Reid**, Founder – Secret Knock

"With a clear eye and courageous heart, Will Craig take us on a journey toward the most significant quest of our lives: finding the path that is truly ours."
~ **Maria Sirois, PsyD**, Author of *A Short Course in Happiness After Loss*

"I'm deeply pleased that Will Craig has picked up the Hero's Journey banner and is continuing to work out its beautiful design."
~ **Christopher Vogler**, Author of *The Writer's Journey*

"Engagingly and intelligently crafted, *Living the Hero's Journey* systematically mentors the unique, inner journey to passion and purpose. An elegant guide for self-discovery and transformation."
~ **David Krueger, M.D.** Executive Mentor Coach and author of *The Secret Language of Money*

"The lessons of ancient mythology and modern movies woven into a tapestry so bold and vibrant, the wisdom jumps right off the page."
~ **Dr. Laura Belsten**, Master Certified Coach

"Applying the Hero's Journey to my own life enabled me to reexamine my feelings for my long departed parents. I gained closure and for this gift, I am eternally grateful."
~ **Brian Sidorsky**, Founder of the University of Success Library - Junior Achievement

"Everyone wants to be a success and *Living the Hero's Journey* is the book that provides the road map you need on your quest."
~ **Don Green**, Executive Director - Napoleon Hill Foundation

Dedicated to Griffin Alexander Craig
~ my son, my friend, my hero.

Live and Learn Publishing
Boulder, Colorado USA

Copyright 2017 © by Will Craig
All rights reserved.

ISBN 978-0-9790448-5-4
Printed in the United States of America

Illustrations: Ignacio Corva–Mar del Plata, Argentina
Editor: Nirmala Nataraj–New York, USA
Joseph Campbell's Hero's Journey schema from *The Hero with a Thousand Faces* (New World Library) copyright © 2008 by the Joseph Campbell Foundation (jcf.org), used with permission.
Christopher Vogler's Hero's Journey schema from *The Writer's Journey* (Michael Weise Productions) copyright © 2007 by Christopher Vogler (thewritersjourney.com), used with permission.
Joseph Campbell and the Power of Myth with Bill Moyers (Alvin H. Perlmutter, Inc. and Public Affairs Television, Inc.) © 1988. Six program DVD series available from Athena Learning (athenalearning.com/power-of-myth-25).

CONTENTS

PREFACE
One Man's Quest

It was a promising spring morning at my home in Orlando, Florida, when I woke up ready to rock the world. I had just entered my thirties and was hitting my stride. The grand plan was to retire by the time I reached the big 5-0. And when I say retire, I mean retire "living well."

It seems like I woke up a few days later (or was it a few decades?) and I was 60 years old. What? All I could think was, *When the heck did this happen?*

Still half asleep, I stumbled into the bathroom. I flipped on the light, squinted into the mirror, and saw my father squinting back in my refection—scared the crap out of me.

I paused to check out the wrinkles and sun spots I had never seen before. I still couldn't figure out where the time had gone. I didn't feel like the man in the mirror. Inside, I was still in my thirties. Okay, maybe forties. But 60? You gotta be kidding me! There must be some mistake.

So, what happened between that spring morning of possibilities and that scary day in the mirror?

Decades had flown by like I was on autopilot. My daily routine consisted of putting out fires, scrambling to appointments, and taking out the trash. My nice, neat plan was a mess. It was hardly recognizable and much less realistic. Sure, I had reached many of my goals, but so much had changed— including my dreams. Not only had the deadline for the grand plan come and gone, but it wasn't what I wanted anymore. My expectations for "living well," and what that meant, were different. It's not that I wanted more. In fact, I wanted less, but I wanted the less to be better.

I shared my quest with a good friend who told me I was living the "Hero's Journey." What? Hero? No, that wasn't me. I was just a regular guy doing the best I could with what I had. The closest I came to being a hero was when I went to the movies and quietly slipped into the role of the main character.

My friend explained that the Hero's Journey is a narrative structure for storytelling that pre-dates the Greeks and Romans. The mythological framework has transcended time and cultures. The myths of today are told by Hollywood screenwriters using the Hero's Journey as a template for developing interesting characters, plots, and impossible situations.

It turns out, I've been on the adventure of a lifetime—one man's quest for living well. Coming to appreciate the metaphors in mythology and the magic of the movies helps me envision my path. I'm able to make better sense of the sometimes-confusing map of life while living the Hero's Journey.

WHY ME, WHY NOW

Why am I writing this book? Because I need to take this journey with you. I want to understand what is happening in my life. I want to acknowledge and appreciate the ongoing tests and trials I face instead of resenting them for being disruptive and inconvenient.

Am I responsible for everything that happens to me? Better yet, am I making my life unfold this way without even realizing it? What can I do to make it better? What needs to happen, right now, for me to author my personal myth—the story of a life well lived?

We're on this journey together because, as author Richard Bach explains, "We teach best what we most need to learn." The research and reading, the insights and investigations, are all leading me down a path that is strange and new, yet eerily familiar.

I don't have all the answers, and this is not a "how to" book. In other words, you're not going to receive a to-do list on how to live your life. There are no "shoulds" and "musts" here. I only hope to transform some knowledge and information into experience—an experience that enables you to bypass many of the obstacles while developing and honing your own guidance system.

For me, the process is as frustrating as it is exciting. Even as I write this book, I find myself deleting, rewriting, and replacing often. Sometimes entire sections get tossed because—in a fresh light—they seem irrelevant or redundant to what's already been explored. Still, in the dark, I trip over new discoveries that enlighten the journey. Discoveries like: Life isn't easy so why am I expecting it to be? And, if I am the hero of my life, I better start acting like it.

I encourage you to combine the passages that resonate with you and what you already know to be true in your heart and soul. Build your knowledge base, as I'm attempting to do, and gain experience that will garner you wisdom. We're in this together. I am your adventure guide and loyal ally for the entire quest.

INTRODUCTION
You Were Born to Flourish

In an age where people look outward for direction and upward for inspiration, *Living the Hero's Journey* provides a time-honored template for looking inward and going deep for the answers we all seek. By using ancient mythology and contemporary storytelling as the bifocals through which to envision our future, we have the opportunity to explore what we have known on a cellular level since the dawn of time: In myth there is magic.

First revealed by mythologist Joseph Campbell, the Hero's Journey is a ritual of storytelling handed down from generation to generation, taking on new forms and multimedia formats. In fact, the Hero's Journey is in our genes—good and evil, love and loss, life and death. In this book, we are living that journey on a quest for personal growth and development. We are hardwired for adopting and adapting to the challenges of life, and for deciphering and discovering our destiny. At our best, we are living the Hero's Journey.

Stow your gear, as we are embarking on an actual Hero's Journey—not an outbound voyage around the world, but an insightful exploration of the landscape of our inner being. When we charge off on our action-adventure, we will encounter supernatural forces, transform ourselves in a decisive victory, and return home to share the elixir of life.

Not many people have the awareness, much less the courage, to set out on such an ambitious expedition. "If the genuine way was simple and easy," says author Michael Meade, "no vision would be required, no dream would be needed, and no one's soul would be truly tested." True happiness—and maybe more importantly, fulfillment—is experienced not at the end of the journey, but while following our path. If we cannot find joy in the journey, there will be no delight in the destination.

Living the Hero's Journey is a fresh start with a new perspective—a map of self-discovery for discerning our destiny. Living one's life through the lens of the Hero's Journey provides us with a visual representation of our lifelong quest. Envisioning our future becomes tangible and workable. Immersing ourselves in a powerful visual metaphor affords a birds-eye view of the territory between our ears and in our soul.

Be forewarned that the Map of Self-Discovery will seem vaguely familiar yet mysterious and foreign at the same time. Our journey will come with many tests and trials, coupled with our fair share of allies and enemies. We'll not only meet our demons and dragons but get to name them. Recognizing the dragon that has held us back—the one that breathes fire in our mind—has dominated our subconscious thinking long enough. Naming our dragon (e.g., self-doubt, fear, conformity) is the first step in taking our power back.

There is much to learn and even more to experience. For now, just know this: You were born to flourish. Trust in the fundamental goodness of the universe, as Michael Bernard Beckwith, founder of the Agape International Spiritual Center, would say. It is all conspiring to support your growth and potential. Rest assured: This will be the adventure of a lifetime.

YOUR ROLE

In Greek mythology and folklore, the hero or heroine was considered a demigod. The countryside in Greece abounds with statues and temples exalting scores of heroes like Zeus, Hercules, Prometheus, Odysseus, Jason, and Orpheus, just to name a few. With the passing of time, the moniker came to refer to individuals displaying courage and the will for self-sacrifice. Today, we are all eligible for acts of heroism.

Fanfare for the common man!

The character archetypes we see in modern films are simply contemporary versions of these ancient myths. In the realm of motion pictures, as in life, the hero is the focal point of the story. The hero archetype dominates top-of-mind awareness in the collective social consciousness. Both male and female power icons headline not only feature films but novels, television shows, and video games. Traditional comic-book superheroes like Batman, Wonder Woman, Superman, and Xena each have individual elements to their unique version of the hero/heroine archetype that are easy to attach to and identify with.

Action heroes come in all shapes and sizes. Some are adventurous—others don't want any part of being a hero. Some are warriors—others start out as weaklings. Some thrive in family settings—others excel as loners. Heroes are not perfect. They have character flaws, quirks, and imperfections. They have their share of vices, suffer from doubt, and experience fear of failure. In short, they're just like you and me.

The essence of what makes a hero a hero, however, is the willingness to serve others and to give themselves to the greater good. Similar to the police officer motto, "to protect and serve," the maxim of the hero is "to serve and sacrifice."

YOUR JOURNEY

The full itinerary of the hero's inner journey is at your fingertips. Each segment is devoted to a distinct stage of the quest. Think of Part I – *Date With Destiny* as our pre-mission briefing. Part II – *Map of Self-Discovery* is a navigational aid to get us to our engagement point. Part III – *Hero's Inner Journey* is where all the action takes place. Each stage details what to expect and what is expected of you.

Date With Destiny
Part I – Myths, Movies, and Meaning

In preparing for the journey, we look inside ourselves and curiously discover the hero within. As the protagonist in *Living the*

Hero's Journey, you explore the power of stories and the improbable relationship between myths, movies, and meaning.

The foundation and structure laid out in Part I reveals a larger truth, and a deeper level of choice. Destiny is not a matter of chance; it is a matter of choice. It is not a predetermined fate but a culmination of how we choose to live our lives. This section helps us discover the hero within and challenges us to truly be the hero of our lives.

Map of Self-Discovery
Part II – The Hero Within

We chart the course by examining the inner self. Ultimately, the answers we all seek are deep within us, and we unconsciously search them out through vicarious immersions in stories of all types.

The meaning of life is personal, subjective, and challenging to pin down. Individually, we all come to terms with this elusive moving target. The absence of meaning and purpose leaves the hero numb and directionless. The Map of Self-Discovery discloses the symbols, metaphors, and rites of passage providing direction and uncovering the ideal path right beneath our feet.

Hero's Inner Journey
Part III – Know Thyself

With a basic understanding of the storyline, the roles being played, and a quick peek at the map, the hero answers the **call to adventure**. The journey begins in the "ordinary world," in the status quo. We seek a treasure only we can discover in a land of both promise and peril.

The hero must leave the past behind and begin a life-changing transformation. After **meeting the mentor** and receiving the necessary training and gifts, the hero makes a **leap of faith** into the unknown.

While the risks and rewards are ours alone, this is no solo expedition. Along the path, we meet friends, allies, and enemies, as well as a protective advisor and mentor. Standing at the entrance to the special world is the threshold guardian. Crossing into the field of adventure requires dealing with this sentinel, who represents the limits of our present sphere of being—our life horizon.

The hero steps into the "special world" and onto the **road of trials** to face tests and transformative confrontations. Without the perils of fate, the hero cannot discover their destiny. Without risk and challenges, there are no rewards and no fulfillment. Slaying dragons, both external and internal, is all in a day's work for our page-turning adventurer.

The hero's shadow will be the biggest antagonist to confront on the journey. The shadow forces the hero to face their mortality, which helps clarify one's role in life and, thus, our impact on the world. The **ordeal** is a metaphor for the reawakening of the hero. In the process, we discover the treasure of enlightened knowledge and are bestowed with the reward of newfound wisdom.

The hero returns to the ordinary world with the treasure of **transformation**. Unless the hero returns with the "elixir" acquired from overcoming their ordeal, they are doomed to walk this way again, and again, until their transformation is complete.

A successful return brings a deep healing and wholeness. The **endowments** bestowed upon the hero are freely shared with the ordinary world. We come full circle to a familiar world through new eyes. The hero recalls their reawakening while living the Hero's Journey and re-dedicates him- or herself to serve, guide, and give.

We understand we do not become the hero of our life by living vicariously. To achieve **life mastery** and be worthy of a life well lived, we must take action, ownership, and responsibility for our choices. Our date with destiny is not about reaching a final destination. It is about how fully we live the journey.

YOUR ENTOURAGE

As with any Hollywood star holding hero stature, you have personal assistants—guides, if you will—traveling with you on each segment of your journey. They carry your moral compass and maintain a proper heading in the direction of your destiny.

While these companions are not official entities of the Hero's Journey, given the epic nature of the task at hand, I don't think you'll mind the company. When I travel around the world, there's nothing I like more than having a personal guide. On this journey, we have personal guides for each segment.

You'll learn more about these advisors along the path. For now, here's a brief introduction:

1. TRUTH: Be true to your word.
2. WISDOM: Learn from experience.
3. COURAGE: Act in spite of fear.
4. INTEGRITY: Walk your talk.
5. CHARACTER: Stand true to yourself.
6. ACCOUNTABILITY: Take responsibility.
7. GENEROSITY: Give more than you take.

We're all here to learn the lessons of life while commingling with like souls on similar journeys. It's not a race to win. It's not a victory to be sought. The only prize is the one you give yourself: renewal, the final stage of the Hero's Inner Journey.

The first and most important change you may experience is that of knowing the hero rises from within. No one else can play this role for you. The hero you are now and the hero you become depend on the personal myths you create for yourself. To attain the good fortune of a life well lived, an auspicious inner journey precedes the tumultuous outer journey on which you now find yourself.

LIFE ISN'T EASY

If you want to take a quick breather from life's demands, relax in the knowledge that we are all in this together in different ways, for different reasons, on different parts of the path. If someone else's life looks easier or better, it just may be because of the eyes with which we view them. They could be part of your lesson. You could be part of theirs.

The truth is, life isn't easy. Don't expect it to be. If it were easy, you wouldn't learn much about yourself. And isn't that the point of the journey? To improve yourself so you can enhance the lives of future generations and leave the world just a little bit better than the way you found it. To go from merely existing on the surface of life to immersing yourself in the depths of a life well lived.

If you're paying attention, the lessons learned pay dividends. Knowing yourself well, understanding why you are here, and embracing your purpose, uncover the path you are meant to follow. Sharing your gifts and talents, harmonizing with the world around you, and living from the heart smooth the bumps along the way. It's not easy but it is rewarding.

Welcome to the adventure of a lifetime: living the Hero's Journey.

PART I

DATE WITH DESTINY

MYTHS, MOVIES, AND MEANING

John and Jane share a marriage that has become less than exciting and more than predictable. Negotiating the landscape of life has slowly transformed their love into more of a business arrangement than a marriage. Their once incendiary sexual chemistry now barely simmers on the back burner.

You might say John and Jane Smith are your average married couple, living ordinary lives in a garden-variety suburb, working ho-hum jobs. But each is hiding something that marriage counseling isn't going to fix. Secretly, they are both highly skilled assassins totally unaware of each other's expertise and cunning. A spark of excitement enters their marriage when they are hired to take each other out . . . and not on a Friday night date. This is their date with destiny.

On their mission to kill each other, they learn much about themselves and more about each other than they ever discovered in five or six years of marriage. The Smiths take the concept of a marital spat to a whole new level as they fire insults and accusations while shooting their house to shambles. In the end, love prevails. And together, Mr. and Mrs. Smith fight for their marriage by fending off an army of bad guys, bullets, and bombs. The ongoing sessions with the marriage counselor don't hurt, either.

The heroes of this movie are Mr. & Mrs. Smith (Brad Pitt and Angelina Jolie). This action-adventure film was a box-office smash. For the average moviegoer, however, the film is more than just two hours in the dark eating popcorn. It is a journey of adventure, ordeals, and transformation. The path followed by the filmmakers is a narrative structure known as the Hero's Journey; a template of storytelling that spans the ages.

Mythologist Joseph Campbell called it the monomyth; the one literary element used the world over, with countless variations and a myriad of outcomes. While it may be familiar to think of mythological heroes as being from Ancient Greece, the heroes of today's feature films are reading from the same script—the Hero's Journey.

CHAPTER 1

LIGHTS, CAMERA, ACTION!

A hero is an ordinary individual who finds the
strength to persevere and endure in spite of
overwhelming obstacles.
~ Christopher Reeves (1952–2004)

The Studio of the Universe is making a motion picture about *your* life, and guess who's playing the lead role? You!

You are the hero of your life. Who else could be? Sure, there are those leading men and women in films, books, and television whom you might like to emulate. But in the movie that is *your* life, you're it. You are responsible for what happens—and what

17

doesn't. You decide who gets cast in which roles and even the lines you speak. Ultimately, you determine how well you do at the box office of life.

It may seem odd that we need to explore our role in our own life, but there is more here than meets the eye. How many times have you been someone for someone else and knew you were not being the real you? How many times have you done something for someone else that you knew wasn't congruent behavior for you? Maybe you are in that position right now.

You get to write your own script while immersing yourself in this book. Truth be told, you've been writing it all along. You get to be the *you* who is inside kicking and screaming to get out. The *you* who has always been there without a voice and finally gets to step up to the call. The *you* seeking your date with destiny. Life will never be fulfilling until this happens. Somehow, this doesn't come as a shocking news bulletin to you. You've known this subconsciously for some time now. Today you begin a new journey—a Hero's Journey.

SUMMON THE HEROES

A classic figure of Greek and Roman mythology, the hero is often presented to us as an individual of great strength and skill who faces increasingly difficult challenges and always manages to summon the courage and fortitude to vanquish his enemies and please the gods.

Hercules is one such hero whose strength and fortitude were much admired. He was the strongest of all mortals and even stronger than some of the gods. When the Olympians triumphed over the Giants, it was Hercules who was the deciding factor.

Achilles was a hero with an unusual birth experience. His mother wanted to make him immortal, so she held him by his heel and dipped her newborn in the river Styx. Achilles' heroics came into prominence during the Trojan War, in which he commanded 50 ships. The hero was ultimately killed with a poison arrow that landed on Achilles' heel, the only part of his body that wasn't touched by the waters.

Hercules and Achilles—like all mythological heroes—garnered great strength and skills while facing increasingly difficult challenges. How is this so different from your life? You are constantly bettering your skills and becoming stronger with each increasingly difficult challenge. You are the hero of your life!

Admiring the heroism of others is inspiring and natural. There are no surrogate heroes, however, who can be tapped on the shoulder to live your life—even if you believe they could do it better than you're doing it. In today's armchair society, we tend to look up to our heroes when what we need to do is look within.

Looking within is not something we are accustomed to doing. We live in a culture where meeting our outer needs occurs without much effort. We enjoy extensive public services, a convenient utility infrastructure, and an efficient and streamlined food distribution system. Things just show up for us when we need them. We need water; we turn on a faucet and there it is. We need light; we just flip a switch. We're hungry and want to eat; someone cooks us food and brings it to our table. We want to talk to someone halfway around the world; we tap a few buttons on our cell phone. Our needs are met before we can even register a desire.

It almost seems appropriate, given our on-demand environment, that we look to the nightly news to deliver the hero of the day. It certainly doesn't need to be us. We have outsourced just about everything else in our lives. We can outsource this.

It seems counterintuitive to consider luxuries and comforts as barriers to a life well lived. But are they not numbing us to a sense of adventure, a sense that we can be and should be our best selves—not merely surviving, but living to the highest order?

It's time to step up—to be the hero—and to do it in a meaningful way. We each have a date with destiny that cannot be denied or delayed. Outsourcing is not an option.

19

CHARACTER IS DESTINY

Your role in this action-adventure is that of the hero. Don't be intimidated. Your character does not follow in the footsteps of Achilles, Supergirl, or Ironman. In fact, attempting to chart your course along anyone else's path—no matter how much you admire them—only leads you away from your destiny. Regardless of their perceived super powers, others are no match for your uncommon gifts, talents, and abilities. Uncover your unique brand of heroism, and you will find yourself quickly marching in the right direction. How you interpret and express this boldness of spirit defines your character.

While the hero is the character you play, character is also a determining factor in defining your destiny. The character required here emanates from your essence: your individual nature, who you really are.

Destiny and fate are often presented as predetermined from an outside force and as being unchangeable. It may be easier for some to believe we have no choice. If what we think, believe, and do isn't going to change anything, why bother trying? Ironically, life appears simple when someone else calls the shots, makes the rules, and decides the outcome.

Greek philosopher Heraclitus had a different point of view. He concluded that one's future was determined by his inner spirit, proclaiming, "Character is destiny." The traits, qualities, and reputation you develop over a lifetime directly impact where you land on your legacy.

In the theater, however, Greek tragedies would have none of this. The main character was ultimately challenged by the unforeseen actions of the gods, over which there was no control and no hope. The protagonist was not going to outwit, outplay, or outlast fate. The main character was not a survivor in these plays, as the gods were the heroes.

This was Greece in the fifth century BC. Greek tragedies were an offshoot of ancient rites in honor of Dionysus. Son of Zeus and the last of 12 gods accepted into Mount Olympus, Dionysus was god of the arts and theater. But modern plays, including screenplays, are no longer limited to one of 12 heroes. And heroes are no longer limited to individuals with Herculean strength and Athenian skills.

As the main character—and hero—on this journey, the transformation from who you are to who you will become directly influences your path. The ebb and flow of the deep waters of your soul determine the course of your destiny.

ON THE SHOULDERS OF GIANTS

Discovering your destiny is elusive, at best. As we shall come to understand in the pages that follow, we pursue with a vengeance what is already lying calmly within our grasp. On some level, we all have a sense of destiny. If we didn't, we wouldn't be asking the crucial questions. Wouldn't it be so much easier, though, if we just had someone to ask?

Joseph Campbell once said, "Life is like arriving late for a movie, having to figure out what was going on without bothering everybody with a lot of questions, and then being unexpectedly called away before you find out how it ends."

We are afraid of what we don't understand, and as an "intelligent" species, we're clueless when it comes to nurturing and cherishing our inner life. Going inward and downward—seeking one's calling and searching for meaning and significance—are time-honored practices in other cultures. In our contemporary "more is better" society, spirituality is less appreciated, less valued, and less understood than celebrating the outer displays of success.

Isaac Newton, a true visionary of his time (the late 1600s), was a man looking in many directions for answers to questions most people didn't even know to ask. He is regarded as one of the greatest scientists and mathematicians who ever lived. When accused of stealing his hypothesis of light, Newton offered, "If I have seen further, it is by standing on the shoulders of giants."

We would all do well to stand on the shoulders of those who have come before us. It is where we will find the best view and catch the best wind. Our journey inward will require both.

CHAPTER 2

POWER OF MYTH

*Don't be satisfied with the myths that come before
you, unfold your own myths.* ~ Rumi

Mythological tales are often viewed as something that happened long ago, if at all. Myths, legends, and rituals engender images of history that often harken back to medieval times. Many great stories come to us from this era, including the stories about King Arthur, the folklore related to Robin Hood, and Chaucer's *Canterbury Tales*.

To fully understand and appreciate the power of myth, we follow the man who has blazed the trail for us, mythologist

Joseph Campbell. Throughout his adult life, he read and researched legends and myths from varied cultures and civilizations over the course of human history. To his amazement, they all shared a common thread—a basic pattern or framework that still lends itself to great storytelling. He called the structure the Hero's Journey.

The story of the hero has been told and retold since the beginning of time. Indigenous cultures used the oral tradition. Today the hero lives in every form of media, from literature to television to video games.

The Hero's Journey, as it manifests in various cultures, chronicles the notion that all mystical traditions call men and women into a deeper awareness of the very act of living itself. Myths guide us through trials and traumas from birth to death. These ancient stories have supported humanity, built civilizations, and informed religions over millennia.

Joseph Campbell's fame increased substantially in the late 1970s when George Lucas publicly acknowledged Campbell's influence on his creation of the motion picture *Star Wars*. The two became fast friends. I was first introduced to Campbell's work in a series of discussions he filmed at Skywalker Ranch with Bill Moyers. The interviews were videotaped just before Campbell's death in October 1987 and, as such, exemplify a lifetime of knowledge and wisdom.

The African proverb, "When an elder dies, a library burns," has never rung truer. Moyers' television series *The Power of Myth* was broadcast the following spring and brought Campbell his broadest audience. The scholar and teacher was fittingly profiled in *The New York Times* as "a figure of heroic proportions."

FINDING YOUR PATH

The man who coined the term, the Hero's Journey would be the first to tell you that "the path" has been here all along. *The Hero with a Thousand Faces* reveals that all myths, regardless of time or culture, follow the same basic structure. There are no new stories, Campbell argues, just the same stories retold in new and different ways.

In the hands of talented screenwriters and novelists, the Hero's Journey is a compelling storytelling template. It provides a solid structure upon which to hang dynamic plot points, introduce engaging predicaments, and build a dramatic conclusion.

Many films are based on the framework of the Hero's Journey. *Star Wars, ET, Dances with Wolves, Terms of Endearment, Titanic, Shrek*, and *Avatar* all use the storytelling template of the Hero's Journey.

The template is both a powerful way to look at our lives and a metaphor that instructs us on how to lead an extraordinary, meaningful existence. Metaphors embed wisdom and information within the context of a story. From major motion pictures to bestselling fiction to beloved children's books, the crucial components of myths, stories, and fairy tales are embedded with the magic and metaphors found buried within the Hero's Journey.

But don't expect to see a definitive formula or rigid structure here. The journey would not be enchanting or compelling if it were familiar and predictable. A story that keeps our interest is one we can't anticipate. The same holds true for the Hero's Journey of our personal lives. Often, the path we choose ends up being very different from the path that chooses us. Or, as French poet Jean de La Fontaine observed, "A person often meets his destiny on the road he took to avoid it."

This was my experience. I did so poorly in school I avoided anything thing that looked like formal education. The moment I graduated high school I swore I'd never enter another classroom. Decades later I would find myself embracing an unrecognized and undeclared love for learning. Little did I know I possessed the teacher archetype and the destiny that came with it. In the beginning, I had no one to give me direction and no map to consult. I didn't even know there was a life path to be found. What I did know is that I loved the movies.

The messages, meanings, and metaphors encapsulated in our favorite entertainment mediums are laden with personal treasures for us to uncover and explore. Dig deep enough and you discover wisdom and an understanding of who the true hero is of those stories.

SPIRITUAL WARRIOR

Michael Bernard Beckwith talks about the profound inner search being like an adventure for the spiritually courageous, for those he calls spiritual warriors. In his book *Spiritual Liberation: Fulfilling Your Soul's Potential*, he goes on to say, "It is an inner trek that takes us down a road we have not walked before. It is where nothing is avoided . . . and everything is faced."

Life is full of inner mysteries, turmoil, and uncertainty. Many of the traditions and rituals that supported us through difficult times have disappeared in favor of a more "sophisticated" lifestyle. Rites of passage, sabbaticals, vision quests, spiritual journeys. Who has the time?

The fallout from technological advances, mass production, and the better-faster-more life has come at the expense of our souls. Sifting through the rubble and debris of what our throwaway society considers an advanced culture makes locating our path almost unimaginable, even when it is right under our feet.

Looking to the Hero's Journey grounds us in a simpler time. Standing at the roughly sawn wooden table, we unroll the parchment and examine the map by candlelight. From this vantage point, we see the bigger picture and gain perspective on who we are and why we're here. Plotting our course into the unknown is invigorating, even if it means there's a chance we'll fall off the edge of the Earth. Especially if there's a chance.

Learning about what makes us tick enhances our ability to self-motivate, self-manage, and self-respect. We possess the capacity to plan, monitor, and guide a life course confidently determined of our own volition. Understanding our place in the world gets us halfway to making the world a better place.

We won't learn anything new and can't grow or expand if we only stay within the confines of our comfort zone. In the coming pages, we explore the uncharted corners of our inner world to gain new insights and benefit from a modicum of wisdom accumulated along the journey.

THE QUEST FOR MEANING

"Nothing shapes our lives so much as the questions we ask," says author Sam Keen. Can stories and myths answer our burning questions? Possibly. What they can do is help us see our inquisition in a new light. We ask: *What is the meaning of life? Who am I? What on earth am I doing here?*

We are excited, confused, or maybe even frightened by these questions. Nonetheless, as we mature and travel further down the path of our life, we inevitably come to the crossroad where we seek meaning and purpose for our existence. *What matters? How should I spend my life? What do I care about most—and why? Who, or what, benefits from my having been here? What is my fate? Where am I going and how can I get there?* To make these inquiries even more daunting, our high-speed, overly materialistic, mass-confused society redirects and misinforms our curiosity, so we're never quite able to bestow adequate, uninterrupted attention on these age-old questions.

So, where are the answers? Certainly not in school, because these topics are not taught in most—if any—humanities classes. Parents are not equipped with the knowledge or wisdom to teach this at home. What is taught in church and other religious settings seems to be less about what you want or need, and more about what that particular doctrine wants and needs you to believe. So, if not in these traditional places of learning, then where?

Yale professor and author Anthony T. Kronman, believes that we alone—no one else—can answer those questions. They cannot be taken on by another any more than another human being can die for us. In essence, we must do our own living and dying—and a part of that includes asking and finding our own answers to some very fundamental questions about our lives. *Fate and Destiny* author Michael Meade contends that the answers to these questions can be found within the questions themselves, as well as inside the one asking and inside the story already being lived.

While this may not be what we want to hear, there certainly is a ring of truth to it, especially since no answers can be found in the places we traditionally find them. Heroic efforts will be needed to unearth the wisdom we seek.

No amount of personal success, financial freedom, or outer trappings of the good life can substitute for the inner fulfillment of sensing an authentic meaning to one's life. Or, as Meade submits, it is "the knowing that the inner spirit of one's life is aimed at something beyond mere adaptation and survival."

To find satisfying answers to the questions of who you are and why you are here requires going on an inner journey. The quest goes beyond understanding your personality traits, your likes, and dislikes. It goes even deeper than discerning your values and beliefs. Once you begin to recognize and appreciate your overarching purpose for being here, you take command of your true essence. You become capable of delivering your unique gifts and talents to a universe that is just waiting for you to awaken.

PART II

MAP OF SELF-DISCOVERY

THE HERO WITHIN

CHAPTER 3

MAPPING THE QUEST

The greatest prayers are held together with doubt,
and the greatest maps lead directly into the unknown.
~ Michael Meade

Joseph Campbell's framework—which he called a "monomyth"—describes three main "acts" or stages of the journey: Departure, Initiation, and Return. He wrote: "A hero ventures forth from the world of the common day into a region of supernatural wonder: fabulous forces are there encountered and a decisive victory is won; the hero comes back from this mysterious adventure with the power to bestow boons on his fellow man." (Campbell, 2008)

31

In the late 80s and early 90s, Campbell's monomyth was adapted by Christopher Vogler to enhance script development in the motion-picture and television industry. Vogler believed he could translate Campbell's 1949 book, *The Hero with a Thousand Faces*, into movie language and unearth a workable format for enriched storytelling.

While working in the development department for the Walt Disney Company, Vogler had the opportunity to test his theories and refine his structure on the animated features *Beauty and the Beast, Aladdin,* and *The Lion King.* Vogler's subsequent book, *The Writer's Journey: Mythic Structure for Writers,* is not only used by screenwriters who are serious about getting their scripts made into movies, but also by many film schools.

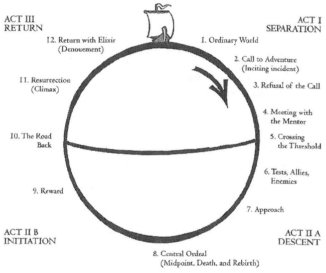

© *Christopher Vogler. Used with permission.*

Vogler modified Campbell's classic mythical journey, updating it for contemporary audiences. Here is the condensed version of the Hero's Journey that has since been embraced by many Hollywood screenwriters.

1. Heroes are introduced in the *ordinary world*, where
2. they receive the *call to adventure*.
3. They *refuse the call* at first, but
4. are encouraged by a *mentor* to
5. *cross the threshold* and enter the *special world*,
6. where they encounter *tests, allies, and enemies*.
7. They *approach the inmost cave*
8. where they endure the *ordeal*.
9. They take possession of the *reward*
10. and are pursued on *the road back* to the ordinary world.
11. They experience a *resurrection* and are transformed by the experience.
12. They *return with the elixir*, to benefit the ordinary world.

So, how might this adventure apply to your life? For a Hero's Journey to fit the criteria and meet the standards of a compelling motion picture, Hollywood veteran script consultant Michael Hauge insists it will be composed of these three elements:

- A captivating or emotionally involving character,
- who is pursuing some compelling desire
- and faces seemingly insurmountable obstacles in achieving it.

Sound about right for your life? Thought so. You're perfect for this role. There's no more need for hesitation or procrastination. Let's get started by pulling out our compass and getting a bearing on where we're headed.

MORAL COMPASS ROSE

Finding our way in this ethically challenged world requires a durable moral compass. These days, the stress test for what's right and what's wrong is extremely elastic. Once again, falling off the edge of the world seems like a real possibility.

For centuries, the fundamental navigational tool for guiding sailors and souls has been the compass rose. Prominent on almost every map, the wind rose—as it was originally called—designates the directions of the 32 winds—the 4 principal winds being North, East, South, and West. When placed inside the circle of a compass, these 32 points resemble a rose in  bloom. The northernmost direction of the compass rose is traditionally marked with an arrowhead or, more ornately, with the symbol of the fleur-de-lis.

If your moral compass is anything like mine it always seems to be swaying from one side of true north to the other. I don't always do the right thing and sometimes I lose my way altogether. My moral compass pulls me back on track. I know I'm headed in the right direction when I'm being true to myself.

Do something totally off the rails and your moral compass will never let you forget. When I was a young adult I participated in a club that was created to help up and coming professionals. The annual election of officers was being presided over by the outgoing president, John—a guy I admired and wanted to emulate.

When all the ballots were collected, he chose me to help him count them and determine his replacement. The two of us retreated to the building's stairwell for some privacy. Sorting through a bucket of paper strips, we placed them into two piles on the floor. It was a close race. Very close. The new president won by a single vote.

John wasn't pleased. The winner wasn't who he thought it should be. We recounted the strips but the numbers came out the same. John proceeded to convince me that his choice would make a better president and since we were only talking about one vote—in the best interest of the organization—we should endorse his recommendation for incoming president. Call it peer pressure, call it misguided youth. Whatever you call it, manipulating the election was wrong and immoral.

I agreed to the unethical behavior to be like someone I no longer wanted to be like. But it was too late. We walked back into the meeting room and announced the name of the newly "elected" president. Some thirty years later, I still recount this incident like it was yesterday. And, no, it's not lost on me that this was an organization for up and coming *professionals*.

ANCIENT MAPS, NEW DIRECTIONS

As long as you're stepping up, you are entitled to the most recent version of the map. We've seen how the Hero's Journey is the primary structure of most myths and many motion pictures. Let's adapt this myth/story/movie structure to characterize the inner journey of personal growth. And while we're at it, let's update the symbology for a more contemporary time.

Let's transition from external to internal. For the purposes of self-discovery, we no longer view this map as a representation of a physical place. We go inside ourselves and uncover what's been there all along. Our destiny.

Going inward, our conscious mind takes the place of the ordinary world (the known). Our unconscious mind, or subconscious, represents the special world (the unknown).

These subtle tweaks enable us to adapt the mythically based Hero's Journey from stories and films to personal growth and development. We can now use the time-tested structure of the monomyth to help us understand ourselves and our purpose on this path of self-discovery.

Inner Journey

The revised multidimensional map is divided into two unequal spheres: conscious and unconscious. The image of the snake eating its tail may seem a bit unpleasant but it is symbolic of the circle of life. The serpent is one of the oldest and most common mythological symbols, and a featured element of some of the oldest known rituals. In Greek, it is known as the *ouroboros* ("he who eats the tail"). It is the symbol of life transforming itself by discarding the past and embracing the future. The snake sheds its skin, one generation after another, to be born again. If it does not renew itself, if the snake is not reborn, it ceases to exist.

In alchemy, the medieval predecessor to chemistry, the ouroboros represents the spirit of Mercury and the cycle of life and death. For an alchemist seeking the elixir of everlasting life, it symbolizes the eternal unity of all things. For us, it unites the conscious and unconscious minds.

While we're here, we should also clear up any confusion about the subconscious mind. Often, *unconscious* and *subconscious* are lumped together as meaning the same thing. I've done it myself. This truly annoys professionals in the psychology community (insert smile here). As a shout-out to them—and as a courtesy to you—I'll do my best to provide a simple and concise explanation of the three minds.

Conscious: According to Sigmund Freud, the conscious mind is populated with everything inside our *awareness*. Everything we're thinking, caring, feeling and fantasizing about. Fortunately, with all of that to do, this is also the only mind with the ability to focus and visualize. It is responsible for logic and reasoning. This is where decisions are made and directives are given. It is the gatekeeper and filter of your belief system. Remembering utility items like your phone number, Google password, and the visual map of how to get work are delegated to the subconscious for instant retrieval when required. The conscious mind is also where we imagine, create, and envision a brighter future. With a workload of this size, it may be hard to believe this is the smallest of the minds. In fact, scientists suggest it represents only about 10% of your brain's capacity.

Subconscious: This mind is responsible for involuntary actions. Your subconscious regulates your breathing, your heartbeat, and dozens of other ongoing functions that run the body. It monitors the sensations of your five physical senses, and some believe it is the origin of a "sixth sense," as well. The subconscious manages recent memories, recurring thoughts, temporary feelings, and the moods generated as a result of these. The subconscious can do so much so fast because it sorts and codes using symbols. It acts as an onboard search engine recalling pertinent facts and responses to any given situation, and then delivers these to the conscious mind. This is how we provide "informed" reactions and "enlightened" responses.

There's a catch, however. The subconscious mind only takes literal commands from the conscious mind. It cannot distinguish true from false, right from wrong, reality from fantasy, or an actual event from one that is vividly imagined. Of all three components of the human mind, the subconscious occupies the most space (50–60%) and is arguably the most significant.

Unconscious: The *source* of all internalized information, knowledge, and experience is the unconscious mind. This is the vault. Deep feelings, ingrained behaviors, and distant memories are filed away here for long-term storage. As such, they aren't directly accessible to the conscious mind. Only the subconscious mind can search and secure this data and—even then—access isn't necessarily guaranteed. You've probably experienced having a memory right on the tip of your tongue but, for some unknown reason, it can't be pried out of the unconscious. There's no backdoor to the unconscious mind. Not even the NSA can access it (although they're probably working on it).

My advice? Just forget it. Literally. Leave it alone and give that troublesome unconscious mind a chance to let its guard down. At a moment when you least expect it, your subconscious will sneak in, retrieve it, and express it to the conscious mind like it came out of thin air.

Isn't it interesting how we depend on the conscious mind almost exclusively for our health and well-being? What we may not recognize is that while our conscious mind calls the shots and decides how we *act*, the unconscious filters our experience and determines how we *react*. File this last bit of information away for later. It is one of the keys to surviving and thriving on our inner journey.

In Michael J. Gelb's book, *How to Think Like Leonardo da Vinci*, researchers estimate that our unconscious mind outweighs the conscious mind by more than ten million to one. Is there any doubt where you'll find your hidden, natural genius? Leaving the conscious mind, we cross the threshold into the special world of the unconscious mind. Let's see how good we are at listening to a part of us that is much smarter than we are.

To keep things uncomplicated and to stay true to our updated simplified map, the subconscious and unconscious together represent the special world in the Hero's Journey and are simply referred to as the *unconscious mind*. The Map of Self Discovery is the Hero's Journey adapted for the purposes of personal development. We'll switch back to the more familiar symbols and analogies later, but for now, let's stick with the key to all successful journeys: self-knowledge.

YOUR WISH IS MY COMMAND

One way to visualize the three minds working together is to recall your last trip to the library. Depending on the size of the library, it can be almost impossible to find the book you're looking for without the help of the librarian.

I like to think of my librarian as the Genie from the animated Disney film *Aladdin*. The Genie character, voiced by Robin Williams, is lightning-fast, has a multitude of options, and he's fun. He has a built-in super search engine to access the massive library of the unconscious mind. Genie does whatever I consciously tell him to do—without question.

The Genie we all have inside us is awaiting our instructions and is ready to grant our every wish. Of course, if it were this easy, we would all live in castles and zip around on magic carpets.

Want to change your life? Here's the quick answer: Pay closer attention to your thoughts and the instructions you give your Genie. If that sounds too simple, just grab your magic lamp and read on.

Sometimes we think the things we say to ourselves don't matter, that they are just random or fleeting thoughts. The fact is, what you say to yourself (your Genie) really *does* matter and will determine your fate for the day, the week, and your entire life.

Where can you find this Genie? He is your subconscious mind. And here's the rub: We don't have an option as to whether or not we give him instructions. He pays attention to our every thought. Our only point of control is the type of instructions we provide.

If you're thinking, "Life stinks, this is really lousy," your Genie hears that. You may not think he is affected by this negative self-talk, but Genie takes it all in and attempts to give you what you have requested. He is very disciplined this way. The trouble is, he's not very good at deciphering moods, doubts, and fears. In fact, your Genie has no reasoning capabilities whatsoever. That comes from your conscious domain. His only job is to obey your commands.

When you tell yourself, "Today is going to be a bad day because that's the way my 'luck' runs," your Genie hears that and says, "Okay, I have received your wish. Here is your bad day!" Of course, you didn't mean for him to take what you said literally, and you may not have even realized you used up a wish when you had that thought.

Think about the last time you balled up a piece of paper and threw it across the room into the trash can. Bull's-eye! It feels so good to make a shot of that distance with deadly accuracy that you decide to do it again. This time, you give it some thought. That little nagging part of your brain you thought was asleep starts telling you, "That first shot was luck. You can't do that again." And sure enough, your next shot bounces off the rim onto the floor. You immediately spring up and grab the wad of paper, not dropping it in the trash but taking it back to the spot from where you missed to try again. We've all played the trash-can game. It's also an excellent example of Genie executing the commands we provide him.

We must be very careful what we tell ourselves because our Genie, as wonderful as he is, cannot distinguish our real intent. Everything we say passes to him without going through any filters. We may tell ourselves, "This is stupid. I'm not going to try very hard to do my best because I'll probably fail anyway." Our intent may have been to give ourselves a cushion to fall back on just in case we didn't do as well as we'd hoped. The trouble with giving ourselves that out is that Genie will do everything in his power to grant our request of failure. He is undermining our ultimate desire to be the best we can be. He doesn't mean to do this, of course; he is just following the orders we gave him.

We all have this magical power. Sometimes we don't even know it, much less take responsibility for it. We tend to pay more attention to the events in our lives. When we react to something that has happened to us, we label it and then attach a story to it. Good, bad, exhilarating, depressing, rewarding, or unfair, we make a note of it. We give these stories to our Genie for safe keeping. He stores them in the unconscious and will dutifully recover these accounts of events just as you have filed them. When we come to a similar event in our life—sometimes years after Genie first filed the original story—he quickly provides us with the immediate reaction to take on our current dilemma based on this historical precedent.

At first glance, this sounds well and good. You have a living encyclopedia at your disposal along with your own Genie librarian to tell you the correct response in any given situation. The challenge associated with this repository of stored responses is that many times those responses are out of date and overdue for a change. We may have matured and outgrown a conditioned response, yet we continue to engage in inappropriate, self-destructive behavior, simply because we have programmed ourselves to do so.

Our lives today are the culmination of every thought we've ever had. Once we embrace this concept—once we recognize we have created our world and take responsibility for it—we also realize we have the power to change our world by simply changing our thoughts. We can rewrite our story through new experiences and different responses, and enjoy a renewal of our inner lives.

REVIEWING THE MAP

Joseph Campbell's original Hero's Journey—along with Christopher Vogler's masterful adjustments and fine-tuning—provide a useful template for our inner journey. As we overlay the elements of personal growth and development, a fascinating Map of Self-Discovery reveals itself. The map discloses the symbols, metaphors, and rites of passage that provide direction and expose the ideal path right beneath our feet.

Following this route requires the use of our moral compass. Living an authentic life and following our true north is not always as simple as it seems. The testing of our values, principles, and boundaries is endless. Ironically, the biggest enemy we face comes from within.

The information and experience you feed your mind(s) determines the quality of your life. If you want to change your life, change your thoughts. What you say to yourself (your subconscious) truly does matter, and your zany subconscious librarian will take your every thought literally. Life is challenging enough without sabotaging yourself. Think well.

Behold the Journey That Awaits You
Personalize a full-screen, interactive version
of the Map of Self-Discovery
at: willcraig.com

CHAPTER 4

CIRCLE OF LIFE

*It's the circle of life, and it moves us all, through
despair and hope, through faith and love, 'till we
find our place, on the path unwinding.*
~ Elton John, "Circle of Life,"
from *The Lion King*

Within just a few months' time, the hero character of *An Officer and a Gentleman* comes full circle, a changed man. Zach Mayo (Richard Gere) meets Marine Corps Gunnery Sergeant Foley (Lou Gossett, Jr.). Zach is the officer candidate and Sgt. Foley, the berating drill instructor. The 13-week program is designed to weed out those unfit to become an Ensign in the U.S. Navy.

43

Sgt. Foley believes Zach lacks motivation and is not a team player. He bullies and torments the young candidate, trying to get him to drop out. Zach refuses. In a moment of frustration, distress, and total exhaustion, Zach finally admits he has no options in civilian life. This pivotal self-realization is a major turning point for Zach, and he commits to becoming an officer and a gentleman.

After completing his training and attending graduation ceremonies, Zach—still in his dress whites—rides his motorcycle back to the training area. He watches Sgt. Foley, his former nemesis (and mentor), berating a fresh batch of officer candidates. One kid in particular is getting the brunt of Foley's wrath. Zach listens to the same speech in the same tone at the same volume that he had personally received just weeks earlier.

Ensign Zach Mayo smiles, turns, and rides off.

Life is a circle. We come back around to some of the same places we've been before, literally and figuratively. With a modicum of hope, we have grown into a better human being. If not, life has a way of sending us around the same loop again until the lesson—and the growth—is complete. The end of one journey transitions us to the next. We may not look much different, but we are not the same person we were before. We change whether we choose to grow or not.

AWARENESS, CHANGE, RENEWAL

We continue our transition from the external world to the inner world; from the ordinary and special worlds to the conscious and unconscious.

In place of the three main external segments of the Hero's Journey (*departure, initiation, and return*) let's overlay *awareness, change,* and *renewal* to reflect better the personal growth we seek. The three main segments of the inner journey take us through not just our lifelong expedition but the cycles through mini-journeys, hikes, and crossings along life's path. Each adventure begins as it always does—with awareness.

Three Stages of the Inner Journey

Awareness: Our experience of *awareness* happens at the conscious level. Once we experience something (good or bad); once we garner new information; once we become mindful of something we had previously been clueless about (an issue, a threat, a toleration), we reach a crossroads. We have a choice. We can choose to ignore and remain as we are and where we are. Or, if we decide to grow and develop, we can take action.

Change: Once we fully commit, *change* begins happening at the unconscious level. We make a leap of faith into the unknown. There we find familiar friends and new allies, as well as new challenges and old enemies. We experience numerous tests and trials along our personal path. Setbacks and failures are seemingly abundant. Pushing through the ordeal, we transform and come full circle, possessing newfound wisdom, gifts, and talents.

Renewal: With a bounty of inner treasures, we begin our return to consciousness. This is no time to let down our guard, though. The elixir we have worked so hard to secure could be snatched away. We have an opportunity to make the most of the reward that is part of us now. Having survived the ordeal and completed the transformation of change, we ignite the torch and become light bearers for those who follow. With the sharing of our gifts of knowledge and experience at the conscious level, our *renewal* is complete.

Undoubtedly, the most challenging part of the journey is change. It requires abandoning the status quo, however mundane, in favor of taking a leap into the unknown. The hope of renewing our spirit puts our souls at risk. Do we have enough fire in us to persevere? Do we have what it takes to complete the journey?

On the reality-television series, *Survivor*, host Jeff Probst tells contestants at Tribal Council, "Grab a torch. In this game, fire represents life. Once your fire is gone, so are you." The flame that burns in each of us requires that change is the necessary accelerant for renewal.

Change doesn't come easy, nor is it quick. The bigger the request, the tougher the challenge and the longer the timeframe. We know we want to be better at this game of life and have our flames burn brighter.

It's good to keep in mind that when an object burns, something is eliminated. Light a candle and eventually the wax disappears. No more candle. Light a fire on a cold winter night, and in the morning, the burning logs that kept you warm are gone. Changing—and thus eliminating—unwanted behaviors, unhealthy habits, and unnecessary drama is a good thing. However, losing a part of ourselves, regardless of how much it needs to go, can still be tough.

We say we'll do anything for this abundant reward. But do we fully understand what we're committing to? What price are we willing to pay? What or who will we leave behind in the process—possibly in ashes?

Change is the currency of a life well lived. How are you spending yours?

This is tough stuff. If change were easy, everyone would do it. Most don't. One thing many people do not realize is, if they don't embrace change or at least accommodate it, they are doomed to repeat the path, rerun the race, re-learn the lesson. We all have the option to renew or redo.

In the film *Groundhog Day*, Bill Murray's cynical and arrogant weatherman character, Phil Connors, relives the same day over and over again in the town of Punxsutawney, until he gets it right. Every morning his alarm brings him into *awareness* to repeat the previous day. Phil is trapped in an endless time loop until he re-examines his life and is willing to *change* to become a better person. Once he does, Phil experiences a sense of *renewal*, and life improves dramatically, not only for him but everyone in Punxsutawney.

The metaphor here is direct and to the point. While we may not get to redo a day that didn't go the way we planned, we do have the opportunity to improve our lives incrementally one day at a time.

This is life, and it takes time (thank goodness). We are restless beings. As much as we fight change on a conscious level, we all want and need it. Somewhere deep down, we know this is why we are here. Enjoy it while you can—even the tough parts . . . especially the tough parts.

We have a choice: We can wallow in how unfair and hard life is (and be totally justified)—or we can choose to master this part of the inner journey and firmly grab hold of the elixir of life.

STEPS ALONG THE PATH

Those who can't or won't change become stuck in what Thoreau calls "lives of quiet desperation." They know they should stand up and answer the call, but instead, choose to remain seated and suffer quietly in mediocrity (usually with a can of beer, a bag of chips, and the remote control).

In nature, change is a constant; without it there is death. If you're not growing, you're dying. If you *are* growing, you're changing. Embrace the unknown; it is only there you will find your treasure.

Hero's Inner Journey

In the context of personal growth and development, here are the stages and steps of the inner journey. A Map of Self-Discovery, if you will.

AWARENESS   Call to Adventure

Meeting the Mentor

Leap of Faith

CHANGE   Road of Trials

The Ordeal

Transformation

RENEWAL   Endowment

Life Mastery

With heightened *awareness*, we observe a *call to adventure*. We quietly tolerate the status quo until we can no longer resist the signs and sirens of the call. We move forward along the path regardless of how many times we've previously refused the call. We commit to *change* and prepare to make the leap into the unknown, our subconscious mind. We gain insights and tools when *meeting the mentor* that assist us down the *road of trials* and through the *ordeal*. Along our life path, we also encounter unlikely allies and longtime enemies. Many setbacks, some temporary success, and countless failures trigger a subtle process of *transformation* that brings us closer to the person we know, at least subconsciously, we can become. Harvesting this knowledge and wisdom provides the *endowment* of gifts and talents to share with others in the known, conscious world. Our *renewal* provides us with fresh eyes and enables us to envision expanding our success to a place of *life mastery* and meaningful significance.

This is the Hero's Journey. And it's not just one lifelong journey. Our lives are composed of numerous circumnavigations around the Map of Self-Discovery. Each revolution is an evolution in our growth. Some trips take a short time; some take longer. Other expeditions bring about exciting change while still others grow us exponentially. Then again, some quests leave us with nothing, and we must begin again. They are all different. They are all lessons along your life path.

CONCENTRIC JOURNEYS

One excursion within my lifelong journey has been my formal education. For the first third of my life, I didn't have much. At 16 years old, I barely graduated from high school and was thrilled I would never have to learn another thing. (I was a teenager. I already knew it all!) I wouldn't stumble into my first college classroom for another two decades.

I title this chapter of my journey "Education Interrupted."

The story I created for my life, up until I was 36 years old, was that I wasn't very smart. Growing up, I hated school. My high-school guidance counselor flat out told me I wasn't college material. That was all right with me. And it didn't hurt my dad's feelings, either. We couldn't have paid for it, anyway.

The two decades that followed found me comfortable with that story, if not somewhat unfulfilled. It took me 20 years to realize I had the power to change my life, to write a new chapter, to alter the direction of my story altogether.

I was the executive director of a nonprofit youth program. Most of the educators under my direction had master's degrees (*awareness*). Ironically, they were being led by a guy who barely made it out of high school. I felt like a fraud. One day I finally shared my embarrassment with Robert Smith, the program director (*mentor*). He told me I could easily solve this problem by going to college. I laughed and said, "I'd be 40 years old by the time I graduated." He said, "Will, in four years you're going to be 40, anyway. The only thing you need to decide is whether or not you want a college degree" (*change*).

So, that's what I did. And, you know, it wasn't that bad. It turns out I had some smarts, after all. I've since written chapters into my life I didn't believe possible (*renewal*). I even went on to earn a master's degree in—of all things—education.

Here's another example of a mini-trek. It might seem like a mundane issue in the larger scheme of things—that is, unless you're living it right now. You've been butting heads with a co-worker since the first day you met in the conference room. It's not a life-or-death ordeal, but this situation needs to be different or it's not going to end well. The *awareness* has been with you since the beginning, and now management has you co-leading a new project team. You've been resisting the *call to adventure* to develop a manageable working relationship with this person. You must now make a *leap of faith* into the unknown and commit to change. Ready or not.

The next few weeks are an *ordeal*. Disagreements, discouragement, and disconnection rule the days. Each of you is demonstrating passion for your position, competing to do what you think is best for the company.

Despite the awkward dynamics, the project is coming together. The leader of another team casually drops by to take a dig at your team and, in particular, your management style. Surprisingly, your co-lead immediately jumps to your defense and compliments your leadership abilities. You're blown away. You find yourself speaking highly of the same co-worker who— up until two minutes ago—was a pain in the ass.

A spark ignites something unforeseen. The two of you look at each other differently now. Not only do you realize you share the same love for your work, but a new passion for each other is quietly emerging (or maybe not so quietly). This sudden *transformation* changes everything. The revelation of what the two of you can do together is electric. This unexpected detour has magically morphed co-workers into cohabitators. The warm reward of falling in love creates more of the same. Sharing the *endowment* of your gifts and talents in this newly forged relationship benefits everyone you touch. Already, new *awareness* is developing as you both glow in this beautiful state of *renewal*. Who knows where that path leads from here?

CIRCLING DESTINY

Each mini-journey within the lifelong journey brings us closer to mastering our worlds. Completing each smaller rotation falls within the larger orbit of our life trajectory. Each expedition into the unknown provides a galaxy of opportunity for a brighter, wiser, and more glorious version of ourselves.

Mini-journeys happen over a period of time: Your time away at college, raising your kids, the years in a past marriage, that summer volunteering, your first career. The events in our lives have a way of segmenting themselves when we take a birds-eye view of them—unlike when we were living them and everything was in our face. We couldn't see much beyond the challenges of the moment.

It's helpful to revisit past mini-journeys. We gain an understanding and appreciation for the sacrifices made and lessons learned. The Map of Self-Discovery helps us reconcile the seeming randomness of our lives. By documenting the awareness, change, and renewal aspects of a previous journey, we are granted insights into their purpose and why we needed to follow that path during that time. The value in this exercise comes in the quality time you spend wandering through your memory banks.

Looking back, we grasp the significance of life's lessons. Going forward, the map is a guiding metaphor for our quests.

If it seems like the turmoil, trials, and tribulations never seem to end, you're right. This is true for everyone, regardless of how wonderful other people's lives seem compared to yours. Those with more money than you (and there always will be) have just as many ordeals to contend with as you. Those ordeals are different in nature, of course, but every bit as challenging for them.

People who are less fortunate than you (and there always will be) may be grateful not to have the life lessons you need to learn. They, too, have a rocky path to travel. Some people are smarter, better, and faster than you (and there always will be), and none of that matters.

You're not going to win the game of life. When the game is over, so are you.

You're not going to lose, either. Life isn't a competition (although it's easy to see why many think it is). Expect that it's going to be tough—so be ready for those fortuitous curve balls. The role of the hero is to serve and to sacrifice. Do you want life to be easy, or do you want it to be meaningful?

Know that your only guarantee is that you will be tested and challenged as every hero is. So, tell the universe to bring it on. That's better than sitting on the couch waiting for something to happen.

EVOLVING SELF-DISCOVERY

The stages of the hero's inner journey include awareness, change, and renewal. We become aware of a need for change and can consciously accept the call for change, or we can refuse the call. Taking ownership of the need for change plants the seeds for growth and renewal in our subconscious.

Within the larger Map of Self-Discovery—the circle of life—there are many smaller circles representing shorter treks, hikes, and expeditions. Each follows the same blueprint of personal growth, providing the building blocks of courage and character.

Resisting change is natural. Just know that if you refuse the call, you are doomed to repeat the lesson. Nature is relentless in its need for change and renewal. Human nature is no different.

Life is the proving ground of an evolving soul.
༄

Life is not a competition. You will, however, be tested and challenged. Life is the proving ground of an evolving soul.

Immerse yourself in the process and embrace the rites of passage. You are the hero of this exciting action-adventure, and the cameras are rolling.

CHAPTER 5

ROLE OF A LIFETIME

You cannot dream yourself into a character;
you must hammer and forge yourself one.
~ Henry David Thoreau

You are the hero of this action-adventure called life—a role only you can play. Not only are you starring in this mythical motion picture, but you are also the writer, producer, and director. Your creative skills know no boundaries on this set, so create the life you truly want and deserve.

The three-act structure previously outlined (awareness, change, and renewal) is the format of the story and the map of your journey. How you choose to travel, the paths you take, and the cast of characters you assemble are yet to be determined. In one of William Shakespeare's most frequently quoted passages, he compares the world to a stage and life to a play:

"All the world's a stage,
And all the men and women merely players;
They have their exits and their entrances;
And one man in his time plays many parts . . ."

Actors in Greek dramas would put on masks. Our *persona* (the Latin word for mask) is the appearance we present to the world. The character we play in the ordinary world responds to the demands of a situation and the environment. Some of us turn this mask, or false front, into a complete set of protective armor. This facade, however, is not the inner personality of the hero.

Taking off the armor and dropping our persona leaves us vulnerable and exposed. Our identity protects us from experiencing pain, from possibly reopening a childhood wound to our ego. But there is a downside. Our persona also keeps us from being who we really are, living in our essence, living from the heart.

The roles we play or masks we wear on the stage of life are partly our own and partly inherited. Roles are a personification of recognizable traits—giving human characteristics to typical patterns of behavior. The roles we see in movies and stories that endure and resonate with audiences are known as character archetypes. We immediately know who the hero is in action-adventure films. He is the one trying to save the world, his family, or a way of life.

Heroes are easy to spot because they are always trying to do the right thing despite the injustices waged against them: Sigourney Weaver in *Alien*, Matt Damon in *The Bourne Identity*, Jennifer Lawrence in *The Hunger Games*. Familiar characters in myth and fiction are essentially archetypes. They help us quickly understand the players without hampering the action or bogging down the storyline.

In its simplest definition, an archetype is a pattern from which copies are made. The origins of archetypal theory date back as far as the Greek philosopher Plato, who called them ideal forms. In his hypothesis, Plato saw these mental forms as imprinted in the soul before it was born and embodying common fundamental characteristics.

The term archetype, as used in psychology, began with Swiss psychologist Carl Jung, who suggested that archetypes comprise psychological patterns derived from historical roles in life that predate the individual. This finding was the genesis of the *collective unconscious*, a term he coined in the early 1900s.

The award-winning film *Avatar* artfully explores the collective unconscious. The Na'avi, who are blue indigenous people of the moon Pandora, are all interconnected. The enormous Tree of Souls serves as a living, tangible form of the collective unconscious that provides access to these imprints and memories.

In Jungian theory, the collective unconscious is the repository of all symbols and experiences of religion, spirituality, and mythology. These are archetypal images ingrained in our understanding before birth, and they become the conceptual patterns behind all our thinking and beliefs. The tricky part is that the shared experiences of our ancestors are not directly knowable and, therefore, require a leap of faith. Don't be concerned; we'll learn how to decipher these unknowns once we're underway. It may be comforting to know that archetypes have been present throughout history and are found all over the world.

CENTRAL CASTING

Much work has been done in the area of casting the action-adventure by Hollywood veteran Christopher Vogler, best known for penning *The Writer's Journey: Mythic Structure for Writers*. In the book, he details the narrative structures and character archetypes now used extensively in successful films and TV series.

Universally present in everyone, archetypes are impersonal patterns of influence. They become personalized, explains *The Language of Archetypes* author Caroline Myss, when they are a part of your individual psyche. Archetypes take active roles as guardians and inner allies, alerting you when you are in danger and guiding you through the unfamiliar or unknown.

Myss goes on to explain that archetypes are universal patterns of power. You have been using pattern recognition all your life to organize your thoughts and emotions. Archetypal power is also the means by which you assess and characterize every person you meet.

In our personal exploration of self-discovery—the objective of this adventure—familiarity with archetypes is vital to the process of understanding our purpose and discovering our destiny. It will be interesting, not to mention revealing, to meet the following cast of supporting characters on the journey:

Hero
Shadow
Mentor
Herald
Threshold Guardian
Shapeshifter
Trickster
Ally

The hero has already been cast in this unpredictable story. Kudos to you, by the way. No one else was even considered for the part. Before you begin celebrating, please know, per your contract, that you have the option to choose several of the other characters on your journey. However, the remaining cast is predetermined.

It's not that you don't know these predetermined characters. You know them all too well. Sometimes they argue with you (your conscious mind). Other times they fight with each other. Sometimes you feel guided by an unseen hand. Other times, abandoned and on your own. You never know when they will appear or what they might say or do. So, prepare to encounter monsters and demons, guides and teachers, seducers and betrayers, mates and masters (some playing dual roles).

It's understandable if you are having second thoughts right now. The hero is going to be a challenging role, to put it mildly. In fact, it's going to require you to step out of a dated character you've played for years—maybe even decades. There is an undeniable comfort and familiarity to the part. You may be so good in this role that everyone believes this character is really you. You might even buy into it yourself. You've outgrown it, though, or you wouldn't be in the place you are right now, searching for answers.

It's time to grow, stretch, and transform. If you maintain the status quo and play it safe, you will be settling for mediocrity gift-wrapped in a dull existence—like the sitcom actor who has been playing the same part for too many seasons who sabotages his success with excess. You've been typecast for too long now, and it's time to step into a new challenge and accept the starring role of a lifetime:

THE HERO
Role: to serve and to sacrifice

The obstacles and roadblocks heroes face in action-adventure movies are what sell tickets and popcorn. These are components of the visible, outer journey. Who doesn't enjoy the exploits of Indiana Jones in the *Indiana Jones* films, Katniss Everdeen in the *Hunger Games* flicks, or Ethan Hunt in the *Mission: Impossible* films?

The heart of the story—what the hero learns along the way, the relationships cemented, the new wisdom acquired—is what moviegoers find enduring and remember most. And so it is with the inner journey, which requires the moral courage and quiet heroism of doing the right thing even (or especially) when no one is looking.

On the surface, the goal of the outward journey is a visible achievement in reaching the destination or winning the battle. The purpose of the inner journey is internal fulfillment and self-actualization—or becoming all that you were born to be. While the "inciting incident" triggers the outward quest, it is an incessant call from within that provokes heroes to achieve their destiny.

In the classic definition, a hero is someone who gives their life to something bigger than themselves. The journey is one of initiation, of awakening an inner power of spiritual knowing. The mythic hero endures hardships and separation from the clan to enter a strange and unfamiliar world. Facing both external and internal obstacles, the hero confronts fears, as well as external challenges to ensure survival. Conquering the forces rallied against them, heroes emerge as their authentic selves, victorious and empowered. The hero returns to the tribe and shares the rewards of the adventure with all.

"But wait," you say. "What if nobody likes me in this new role? What if I don't like the new part I'm playing?"

When I first moved to Colorado from Florida, some 20 years ago, it was a new beginning. My seven-year stint with the nonprofit youth program was over; my marriage was over, and I was over being who I was at that time. I became keenly aware it was time for change.

I wanted to do something totally different. I wanted to be someone I had never been. I wanted to test-drive new personas minus the binds of conformity. Maybe I took it a little too far by moving halfway across the country, but in Denver I could try on a new me without needing to fit into someone else's expectations. I could reinvent, reinvigorate, and renew my life.

Are you ready to play a new role? It's not too late to reconsider. What you learn, what you experience, and what you bring back from your quest will change you in ways you cannot anticipate. The deep inner work you are about to experience isn't light reading and certainly isn't easy. If it were, you wouldn't be the action hero of your life. You'd be Joe or Josephine Six Pack, kicked back on the couch, watching the tube, not even giving a second thought to contemplating a better world.

If you're not ready for this part, that's okay. Sit it out for now and try to be content with the status quo. Good luck with that.

If you *are* ready, let's seize the day.

DISCOVERING YOUR CHARACTER

With a greater understanding of the Hero's Journey and an overview of the Map of Self-Discovery, let's tweak the questions we asked in Part I and come a little closer to making them workable (and answerable): What is my true purpose in life? What changes must I make? How can I best use my gifts and talents?

As we progress on our path, the questions become more specific and relevant: *Who are my teachers and mentors? What do I need to hear? What can I believe in?*

By the end of this book, our questions may well be more along the lines of: *How can I best serve myself, my family, and my world? What constitutes a life of significance and value? What do I want my personal legend to be?*

You may already have answers to some of these questions. This is progress, but notice how these answers mature, unfold, and transform over time. They may already be a little different from when you first formulated them.

There are those who believe a wise old mentor who already knows the answers lives deep within our souls. But, as we will learn about mentors, they seldom give up their wisdom without making us earn it first.

The quest for meaning doesn't culminate at the arrival of a single destination. Nor will it be found in a treasure chest buried on an uncharted island where X marks the spot. The meaning of one's life is more like a moving target; gaining insights and better understanding results from constant adaptation and incremental adjustments. Meaning evolves and emerges from change.

"Progress is impossible without change," said George Bernard Shaw, "and those who cannot change their minds cannot change anything." From a scientific point of view, it was Charles Darwin who determined, "It is not the strongest of the species that survives, nor the most intelligent that survives. It is the one that is most adaptable to change."

Congratulations on winning the role of a lifetime. Carpe diem!

Learn more about your role in the
action-adventure of a lifetime at:
willcraig.com

PART I

HERO'S INNER JOURNEY

KNOW THYSELF

Our journey is about to begin. At this point, we know as much about the path as we can. We have our map and a vague idea of what to expect. We've gathered our navigational instruments and been advised of the dangers.

On this inner journey, it will be easy to get lost and turned around. You'll recognize signposts along the way, and you will also have personal guides for each leg of the journey. I will stay close by, providing you with ideas, suggestions, and thought-provoking questions to move you forward on your quest.

The first signpost you'll spot at the beginning of each chapter is the *Destination*. This is our intended target. You should know that hitting this target won't be easy. We might totally end up somewhere else, and that's okay. Sometimes it's necessary to get lost to find ourselves. Having a destination, though, gives us a general direction and something to shoot for.

Characters in your action-adventure story are introduced periodically in *Fellow Travelers*. Before their arrival, you'll get a heads-up at each new stage at the beginning of the chapter. These are key players on your inner journey. You'll recognize some of them and, ultimately, identify with all of them.

Personal Guides are new members of your entourage: Truth, Wisdom, Courage, Integrity, Character, Accountability, and Generosity. One by one, they will each join the expedition just when you need them most.

Your guides provide clues along the way emanating from seven basic principles:

1) Be true to your word.
2) Learn from experience.
3) Act in spite of fear.
4) Walk your talk.
5) Stand true to yourself.
6) Take responsibility.
7) Give more than you take.

These principles may seem like "standard fare" self-improvement babble, but there is a reason they keep appearing in our lives. While we are responsible for our Map of Self-Discovery, these guides carry our moral compass. Without this primary navigational aid, we have no center and no core strength to withstand the tests of our character.

Trust in your guides and doors will open for you that you never knew existed. Judith E. Glaser, author of *Conversational Intelligence: How Great Leaders Build Trust and Get Extraordinary Results*, says, "Trust creates the pathway which activates a chemistry in the brain that enables the mind to see around the bend; beyond its normal limitations, and even into the future."

To catch a glimpse of our future, we must first understand the past and where we've come from. At the end of each chapter, we'll *Explore Your Role* as it relates to that segment of the journey. We'll review and reinforce the important subtleties and nuances that shape our destiny.

We'll also dig deeper in our exploration with revealing questions of *Self-Discovery*. It is here we have the greatest chance at uncovering a life lesson to guide us on our path. From this vantage point, we can reframe our worldview, reassess our recent experiences, and reinvigorate our fortitude for the challenges ahead.

CHAPTER 6

CALL TO ADVENTURE

*It is only in adventure that some people succeed
in knowing themselves—in finding themselves.*
~ André Gide

We join our hero shortly before his 11th birthday. He is the only child of James and Lily, who lost their lives when the boy was just over a year old. Our orphan hero has since been living in less-than-desirable conditions with an aunt and uncle who neglect and abuse him. They force Harry to sleep in a cupboard under the stairs, which wouldn't be so bad if their bully of a son would just leave him alone.

Letters addressed to Harry arrive at the house, but his uncle keeps him from seeing their contents. As the letters begin arriving more swiftly—and in greater abundance—Harry's uncle fights desperately to keep the young boy from answering his calling. At the stroke of midnight on Harry's birthday, the Keeper of the Keys, a half-giant named Hagrid, bursts through the door to personally deliver Harry's call to adventure: a letter from Hogwarts School of Witchcraft and Wizardry.

Harry Potter leaves the ordinary world with Hagrid for the magical, special world of Hogwarts. There, he will discover his purpose and passion and, ultimately, his destiny.

In the world in which you and I live, the call to adventure may not be as momentous or magical as Harry's, but it can be as meaningful and memorable.

Destination – *Awareness and Action*

Your ultimate destination is bigger and more involved than mere awareness and action. To finally "arrive" requires multiple stops, challenge points, and—hopefully—safe havens along the way. This mid-journey destination (one of many) is to awaken, become aware, and act on your calling.

Fellow Traveler – *Herald*

The first traveling companion to join you is the herald. The role of the herald is to warn and challenge. The herald kickstarts your journey with the announcement of a call for change.

A piece of information is delivered that jostles the status quo and challenges the hero to answer the call to adventure. The herald's job is motivating the hero to take action, in spite of the fact that "the call" may have repeatedly refused in the past.

The herald is the personification of a call to adventure. A person can serve this function or, just as easily, an event or force can trigger the awareness. A mentor can act as the herald. The call to change can also be heralded through a dream or during meditation, or come from some external event like a close encounter with death, a timely call from an old friend, or reading a poignant passage in a book.

In essence, something deep inside is awakening the hero from an ordinary life. The resulting jolt of energy races through the hero's body, causing vibrations and a heightened awareness that change is not only inevitable but imminent. The herald is calling you to the adventure. It's time to take action.

Personal Guide – *Truth*

Walking directly beside you is the guide of truth. Be true to your word and let your word be true. Continue moving forward. There are seven more legs to the journey, and you will gain a new guide and additional fellow travelers at each transition point.

You've already taken the first step. You acknowledge it is time for change and are preparing to take action and move forward. As William Shakespeare would say, "This above all: to thine own self be true."

Be true to your word and deliver on your promises, especially to yourself. Listen to your inner voice, and heed the advice and counsel of the wiser and nobler you. Respect your needs and desires, and it will become easier to respect the needs and desires of others. Your life improves significantly when you take a chance on being sincerely honest and authentic.

If you're feeling sentimental, look at it this way: "We are all of us born with a letter inside us," asserts novelist and artist Douglas Coupland, "and that only if we are true to ourselves, may we be allowed to read it before we die."

The guide of truth is always with you. Just be sure you're listening from the inside out.

> "The truth will set you free. But not until it is
> finished with you." ~ David Foster Wallace

SUFFERING THE STATUS QUO

The first stage of the hero's inner journey is all about awareness. Some hidden part of us may be hinting at change, seeking a renewed spirit, foreseeing a better future. Let's do a full overview of the awareness stage of the journey. Then we'll talk specifically about the call to adventure—or, for our inner journey purposes, the call for change.

Our baseline is the *status quo*. This is where we are. It may not be pretty or exactly the way we want it but, for better or worse, this is who we are right now in the ordinary world.

Then, we get the call. It could be something out of the blue and totally unexpected. For instance, you're passing by the mirror in your brand-new clothes. You stop with a jolt and turn your back to it. Your conscious mind asks, "Do these jeans make my butt look big?"

Your subconscious knows better than to answer.

And there it is. Awareness has crept into your world. Now, every time you pass a mirror—or glass of any kind—you're checkin' out the caboose to see if the mirror was lying. This is known as the *quiet suffering* phase. You're not going to do anything about it, but it doesn't feel good.

Those same jeans that started this whole awareness mess now make a second call. Having gone through the laundry, it seems tougher than normal to get them buttoned. It must be because the dryer shrunk them. This is known as the *resisting the call* phase. You haven't refused to deal with the issue, but you're not ready to acknowledge there actually is one—yet.

Committing to change takes some help. You start to notice and take heed of weight-loss products and programs. Not because you need to, but because you should just be informed about these things.

The next step is about seeking help and *meeting the mentor*. It need not be formal or cost any money. You confide in a friend, who tells you, "What could it hurt to modify your eating habits a little and join a yoga class? The worst that could happen is you'd feel better."

Now you're ready to cross the threshold and make the *leap of faith* into a weight-loss regime. This won't hurt a bit (insert smile here).

Everything we've talked about so far falls within the awareness stage of the journey. The actual hard work begins on the road of trials in the next stage, which is where real change happens. We'll delve into that in the next part of the book. For now, let's go back to the beginning.

CALL FOR CHANGE

On our inner journey, the aim of the call to adventure is that of a call for change. It is to wake up and shake up the hero within. Becoming aware can be the trickiest part. We don't always hear the call, or see it, or feel it (even if it's attached to a 2x4 upside the head).

In the movies, the call to adventure is usually pretty blatant—Princess Leia's "help me" hologram in R2D2, the treasure map received by Joan Wilder in *Romancing the Stone*, or the flood of letters from Hogwarts to a smiling Harry Potter.

In *Butch Cassidy and the Sundance Kid*, the Herald is "News" Carver, who reads newspaper accounts of the gang's robberies and learns that a super posse has been assigned to hunt them down. In *Beauty and the Beast*, the Herald is an old beggar woman who warns the prince not to be deceived by outward appearances. For me, the call came while watching a PBS television special—an enchanting view into a crystal ball of sorts. No one knows exactly when the call comes, much less who or what will deliver it.

Sometimes the heralding can even be silent. In the (otherwise) black-and-white film *Schindler's List*, the girl in the red coat symbolizes the innocence of the Jews being slaughtered by the Nazis. The scene personalizes the horror for Schindler and challenges him to act in ways that are nothing short of heroic.

Many of us are familiar with the role of the herald because of Greek mythology. Hermes is the great messenger of the gods and guide to the underworld. He is also the patron of boundaries and guardian of the travelers who cross them.

The Romans, craving their own identity (and deities), "borrowed" many of their gods from the Greeks and simply renamed them. Mercury, the messenger, was one of them. They used Mercury's name in place of Hermes, added a few original myths to the legend, and called it good.

For you and I, the call for change could come as a literal knock on the door or from an Animal Planet documentary. It could arrive as a subtle "a-ha" moment in the shower, or a disturbing tap on the shoulder (hopefully *not* in the shower). In whatever form it arrives—mystical or just plain ordinary—it is a wake-up call to rise and shine. It's opportunity knocking, and it may not come this way again.

The hero may have somehow managed to survive an imbalanced life and get by with charm, adequate looks, and a sack full of coping mechanisms. The herald's message makes it simply impossible to get by any longer. The new energy of the wake-up call sparks the hero into action.

You've been stuck in the status quo for too long, and the herald is rousing you to venture out and see what's just beyond your comfort zone. It's time to rise to the occasion and shine like the star of your personal action-adventure film. This is your reality show and the camera is rolling. Don't make it boring.

Until we become aware, we will not hear the call. There are many reasons we don't hear it. We may not know ourselves well enough to recognize it. Even if we do know ourselves, we may not be ready for it. We might not want it badly enough, or maybe we're not sure the call is really for us. However, we want to label it, we're resisting the call.

Well, that doesn't sound great, does it? So, what should we be listening for, then?

The herald doesn't always bellow the official call to adventure through a ceremonial baroque trumpet. Often, the call comes in a much softer, gentler voice. Consummate student of personal growth—and consequently, a master mentor—Oprah Winfrey tells us, "That whisper you keep hearing is the universe trying to get your attention."

The call to adventure is likely to be the shortest part of your journey and the most benign. Given the gravity of many of the other steps you experience around the map, this one seems trivial in importance. Doesn't sound too exciting, does it? Ahhh, but wait—there's more.

There's a good reason an entire section of the book is devoted to the "call." Comedian Steve Harvey told Oprah that the two most important days of your life are the day you were born, and the day you find out why. The call to adventure may be short and sweet, but it is also supremely important. If for no other reason, when you miss your call, there are no other steps to be taken (except maybe the ones that go backward).

SITTING IN AWARENESS

The call is the beginning of awareness. Once we receive the call—whatever it might be about—we can no longer deny the reason it came to us. We can ignore it. We can pass it off as just an abstract, fleeting thought (the first time, anyway). We can pretend we're going to deal with it later. In fact, we don't have to do anything about it.

But one thing is different: The reason for the call has now come into our awareness.

Mentor coach Dr. Jackie Black, draws clients into awareness by asking questions. The twist is, she's not really interested in the answers. The goal is to have them sit and explore beyond the story they've been telling themselves. What if the story is no longer their truth? Again, the answer is unimportant. The goal is the exploration that ensues within the client and the call—a call for change—that may be triggered as a result. Dr. Jackie calls it "sitting in awareness."

Think about this section of the book as an immersion into awareness. Let's explore the many calls you receive, as well as why they might go unanswered, and provide you with some basic tools and knowledge to determine which "calls" are irresistible and which are irrelevant. It's not like you have Caller ID with this.

That's the trouble, isn't it? Throughout the day, we're bombarded with so many calls for our attention. How do we recognize "real and genuine," even if it smacks us in the face?

Why should we care? Because calls open and close doors. And walking through those doors changes everything. At least it did for Helen.

Helen arrives at work one morning, only to get fired from her job. She takes the subway back home, just slipping between the rapidly closing doors as the train pulls out of the underground station. Arriving home, she discovers her boyfriend in bed with his ex-girlfriend.

This is half of the premise of the 1998 movie *Sliding Doors*, starring Gwyneth Paltrow. The other half of the premise is a different version of events. Helen misses making it through the sliding doors and is forced to wait for the next train. By the time she arrives home, the girlfriend is gone, no one the wiser. Outside of losing her job, the status quo is maintained—or so it seems.

The movie continues down parallel tracks into drastically different worlds for our heroine. The film intertwines between the two realities (made the train, missed the train) and explores the "what-ifs" determined by a split second.

The story is intriguing because most of us have thought about what our lives would be like had we walked through a different door at some point. What would be different this very moment if you hadn't sat down with this book? What would you be thinking this very second if you had sat down to check your social media instead? Surely, you wouldn't be thinking about this. How, if at all, does this change your life?

Maybe a lot.

Every decision we make, big or small, alters the course of our lives just slightly—and sometimes by quite a bit. With a fresh sense of heightened awareness, is there a call for change that you've been resisting? Are you quietly suffering about something?

SOUND THE BUGLE

It's the fall of 1981, and I'm about to receive my call for change. I'm on the couch channel-surfing and stumble across the Summer Music Games on PBS. The games are an annual championship competition comprising the best high-school and college musicians from around the country and the world. Talk about herald trumpets.

It looks like a marching-band competition on steroids. The only instruments on the field are shiny brass bugles and thundering drums. The participants call it "drum corps"; the fans call it exhilarating.

I'm taking in the sound, excitement, and sheer power of brass instruments in four-part harmony, accompanied by a precision drum line in cadence with other percussion instruments. I just know that if I were in that stadium sitting on the 50-yard line, I'd be getting my face blown off by a wall of sound. These students are amazing! When the broadcast announcer introduces the corps director, Scott Stewart, it strikes me that this guy can't be much older than me.

When the Madison Scouts Drum & Bugle Corps finish their hair-raising performance to a roaring standing ovation (including one from my living room), I hear the call. It is the call for change. I don't know how or when, but one day I am going to be part of this activity.

I was right. Exactly ten seasons and ten broadcasts later, I became the corps director of Magic of Orlando Drum & Bugle Corps. I held the full-time position from 1991–97. I also served most of those years on the Drum Corps International Board of Directors—one as vice chairman of the board sitting alongside chairman Scott Stewart of the Madison Scouts.

This particular full-circle journey falls under the category of "be careful what you wish for." The volunteer youth activity changed my life. I totally switched careers, spent summers touring North America, and married my ex-wife. Well, she wasn't my ex at the time, but you know what I mean.

Little did I know at the time that I was headed down one of the lengthier road of trials and certainly one of the toughest periods of my life. There was never enough money to operate the nonprofit organization. We were always fighting for sponsorships. There were always mechanical problems with the tour vehicles. But who I am now was engendered in those stadiums and on those practice fields. I wouldn't trade it for anything. The passion for this musical art form was hibernating inside of me all along. Answering the call that fateful day, vibrantly activated another piece of the puzzle that is me.

I sometimes wonder—if I hadn't been channel-surfing that day and caught the PBS broadcast, would I have received the call in another way, or was that a sliding door? Had I not been awake to my passion for music and harmony or mindful of my love of experiential learning, would this path have even opened up? Would an essential part of my purpose have been missed?

What about you? Can you remember specific moments when you received a call to adventure? In retrospect, was there a call you possibly didn't recognize at the time?

REFUSING THE CALL

You see it in almost every movie. This is when our hero has been tapped on the shoulder to step up. Instead of answering the call, justifications are given and excuses are made. "We are plain quiet folk and have no use for adventures," says Bilbo Baggins in *The Hobbit.*

William Wallace (Mel Gibson) is a simple farmer in 13th-century Scotland. He only wants to live in peace, even though the English are responsible for his father's death. Wallace witnesses and endures subsequent injustices, yet remains steadfast in his pacifism. He *refuses the call* to adventure by refusing to fight. Patience and toleration are virtues—until they're not.

It is not until the English magistrate has his wife publicly executed that he takes up the call to lead Scotland into rebellion. This dramatic and persuasive call to adventure is from the Academy Award–winning Best Picture, *Braveheart.*

Each refusal of the call intensifies the need to respond, until the call can no longer be resisted or refused. On a lighter note, in *Groundhog Day*, Phil (Bill Murray) is forced to relive a negative loop cycle until he embraces the call for change to become a better person.

In between high school and college, some students are aware enough and smart enough to take a year off from school. Some backpack across Europe. Others take the time to "find" themselves, or at least get a better sense of who they are and what they want to do with their lives.

I guess I embraced this strategy a little longer than most. Twenty years after graduating high school, I still hadn't gone to college, nor had I seen Europe. I didn't even have a passport. I continued refusing the call. When did I stop refusing the call? When it became too painful to ignore.

"The universe is forever sending out a casting call to us to accept our starring role in an A-list movie," says Michael Bernard Beckwith. "As we sit in our inner screening room observing the moment-to-moment changing scenery of our life, we may wonder what indeed is the part we have come to play on this great stage of life."

KNOW THYSELF

Before screenwriters and novelists pen the first scene, they are totally knowledgeable about at least one aspect of their story. They know *everything* about their protagonist, the hero. They even know things they may never use in the story. If it becomes necessary, however, the "backstory" is congruent with the character. They understand the hero: what motivates her, what scares her, what fills her with purpose and passion.

The quickest way—in fact, the only way—to discover your destiny is to *know yourself*. It might sound trite, but the truth is, we often dismiss the idea of fully understanding who we are. We seldom make the effort because we think we already know ourselves. We're reluctant to take on the task of self-discovery because it sounds like a silly seminar exercise. Maybe we don't explore the depths of our soul because we're afraid of what we might find.

Humanity's quest for self-knowledge spans the ages and the globe. From Socrates to Ben Franklin to *Dirty Harry*, the philosophers and storytellers of each era put their spin on the importance of this two-word dictum. The ancient writings of the Egyptians, Hindus, and Greeks all show that knowledge of the self played a significant role in those cultures.

Know thyself is familiar to most as a Greek aphorism carved into the Temple of Apollo at Delphi. The inscription, located on the wall in the forecourt of the temple, greeted guests visiting the Oracle of Delphi. Pythia, as she was commonly known, spoke for the god Apollo. Her guidance and prophecies made her the most powerful woman in the classical world.

According to Socrates, the most important thing in life is to know yourself. His predecessor Pythagoras felt even stronger about introspection: "Know thyself, and thou shalt know the universe and God."

Plato, a student of Socrates, added another layer to the legend with, "I must first know myself, as the Delphian inscription says; to be curious about that which is not my concern, while I am still in ignorance of my own self, would be ridiculous."

Later, the mythology morphed yet again with Aristotle: "Knowing yourself is the beginning of all wisdom." For me, this iteration is the most meaningful and easiest to remember.

One of America's Founding Fathers, Benjamin Franklin, added, "Observe all men; thy self most." Or, if you just want plain talk, Clint Eastwood–style, "A man's got to know his limitations."

As a timeless concept, *know thyself* also appears in Latin (*temet nosce*) on a plaque above the kitchen door of the Oracle in the *Matrix* films. As with the guests visiting ancient Delphi, Neo needs to first know himself before he will understand and be worthy of special guidance from the Oracle.

If the wisdom of self-knowledge has been around for ages, why don't more people heed the time-honored advice? The process may not seem so fun. Plus, it's hard work. Not to mention you're likely to learn things that don't sit well with you.

You are to be commended, though. Not many people are brave enough to go inward and take on an inner quest. Of course, those folks are on the trip anyway, whether they realize it or not; they're just not actively participating like you are.

So, congratulations! Here's what you win: You know your limitations, as well as where you excel. You're able to see yourself in others and appreciate how others want to see themselves. You gain a sixth sense in evaluating how others might behave in certain circumstances, having firsthand experience of how the process works. You have a more accurate assessment of yourself and how others perceive you. You gain confidence in relationships, recognizing that everyone is an apprentice to life, just like you.

Socrates may have been a tad dramatic when he said, "The unexamined life is not worth living." Given his circumstances at the time, however, he was likely hoping to drive home a final point. Socrates made this declaration at his trial in Athens. He was charged with "corrupting the youth" and "failing to acknowledge the gods." He was found guilty and sentenced to death by drinking the potent and deadly poison of the hemlock plant.

Not examining things too much might seem less painful, but it is the coward's way to a slow and sorrowful life. One can take solace in being a follower: complying with directions and instructions, not having to think or make too many decisions. But if you are to be in charge of your life, you must ask questions, challenge the status quo, and take responsibility for who you are and the person you want to become. Too dramatic? You decide.

If you're somewhat nervous about how much you know—or don't know—about your true self, relax. You're not only in good company; you're halfway to becoming enlightened enough to see over the next ridge. It comes back to awareness and being willing to look at the you down deep and not the you underneath the many masks (and hats) you wear.

Regardless of your apprehensions, begin the process of knowing yourself well or your journey will be fraught with missteps and misdirections. Good places to start are personal assessments. There are scores of personality tests online—some better than others. These profiles sprinkle you with insights and inspire you to think differently. (For insights into Discovering Purpose and Passion, take the assessment at: willcraig.com/gifts)

To fully know yourself is a lifelong journey. Begin by looking inward, and gradually go deeper. Spend quiet time with yourself (as corny as that may sound). Look at your strengths and your weaknesses. Be still long enough to sense the relative silence, and listen to what you might hear for the first time. Review your beliefs and what you stand for. Better yet, consider what or who you would die for. If you're afraid of what you might see and hear, that's all the more reason to look and listen. It is the very strife and struggle of coming to know ourselves that gives our lives meaning and significance.

Ask questions. Look for answers. Ponder the stories you tell yourself and others. Ask yourself: *What am I making up about my life (what lies am I telling myself)? What and who do I really want to become?* If you know yourself from the world inside, you have a much better chance of making sense of the world on the outside.

Know yourself so that when life presents you with enigmas wrapped in anomalies, you already have a good sense of who you are and where you're headed. You will not be derailed by irrelevant chaos or gratuitous noise. You'll know what you value, what's important, and why. This enables you to make timely decisions, enhance your well-being, and make the world a better place. You'll also be in a better place to recognize the call to adventure when you receive it.

If you are courageous enough to travel this path, you will need time and patience. There is no shortcut (unless you work with a mentor). This is the journey, and the reward is a life well lived. The good news is, if you start now, do the work, and gain a heightened self-awareness, life keeps getting better.

EXPLORING YOUR ROLE

In answering the call to adventure, you're committing to a call for change. If things were going to stay the same, would you really be happy?

Agreeing that change is needed is hard enough. Making the change requires a tremendous amount of commitment and perseverance. Surprisingly, the powers you need are easy to secure if you're willing to do the work and embrace the challenges presented to the hero within.

Awareness is a curious tap on the shoulder from your traveling companion, the herald. Once you awaken to the need for change, you can't un-see it. You can deny or refuse the call, but only through quiet suffering.

The herald is a busy messenger. Calls for change are issued on a regular basis from the simplest (fix that darn screen door) to the most profound (am I living my purpose?). Most calls, regardless of the type, are ignored or refused—until they can't be any longer. When the screen door falls off, you have no choice but to fix it, even though it would have only been a minor repair weeks ago.

- Stepping into awareness opens the door to a rewarding inner journey.
- Accepting the call to adventure is committing to change.
- The only way to discover your destiny is to first know thyself.

You are to be commended for answering the call to adventure. Like most things that are worthwhile, however, the process of getting there is a lot tougher and so much different from what we imagine. Regardless of how we think this is going to go, rest assured that it won't be anywhere close to what we envision.

Take comfort in knowing this isn't necessarily bad. What happens next and what happens further down the path will help you reach your potential and meet your destiny.

➤ Self-Discovery ➤

1. What calls for change are presenting themselves to you right now?
2. Are there calls from your past that you have ignored or refused? Do they still tug at you?
3. What stories are you telling yourself? Are they true or simply comforting?
4. Beyond the other roles you play (e.g., parent, spouse, colleague), do you truly know thyself?

CHAPTER 7

MEETING THE MENTOR

"Always two there are, no more, no less.
A master and an apprentice."
~ Master Yoda

When the hero of this next story receives the call, it does, indeed require service and sacrifice. It is the call of duty to serve his country.

Not knowing how long he will be away from his family, he enlists the help of his old friend Mentes to watch over and guide his infant son. This turns out to be a smart move.

Our hero is Odysseus, the King of Ithaca, a Greek island in the Mediterranean Sea. It is the 12th century BC and he has

83

been called to fight the Trojans, who aren't being very nice and are not playing fair.

An oracle from Delphi reveals that the city of Troy (in what is now western Turkey) will fall to the Greeks. Indeed, the city will fall, but the Trojan War will last ten years before finally culminating in one of the biggest "gotcha's" in the history of warfare: the Trojan Horse.

The Greeks have been fighting for years to conquer Troy, but the city is impenetrable. In a last-ditch effort, they build a huge hollow wooden horse, fill it with soldiers, and leave it outside the city gates. The remaining fleet sails off, just out of sight, as if admitting defeat and leaving the spoils of war to the Trojans.

Believing the horse is an offering to the goddess Athena—and not being able to resist such a great toy, after all—the Trojans wheel it inside the gates. In the dead of night, the special-forces unit emerges from the Trojan Horse, and kick butt.

Fortunately, our hero is on the winning side. That's the good news. The bad news is that Odysseus's GPS isn't cooperating, and neither is the rough weather at sea. It will be another ten years before he enjoys the comforts of home.

Back in the kingdom of Ithaca, the citizens are getting restless. Penelope, Odysseus' wife, is doing her best to raise their son, Telemachus, and keep the many suitors at bay. By this time, most assume that the king has been killed in the war and that Penelope should re-marry, if only because this gives a lucky suitor an instant crown and direct control over—well, just about everything, including Telemachus, the would-be king.

The beautiful Penelope is hip to this and tells the supplicants directly, "I know you just want me for my crowning endowments—now scram."

As the years pass, the suitors grow in number and impatience. It won't be long before the kingdom is lost. Telemachus refuses to believe his father is dead and sets off to find him. The loyal Mentes' expertise and competence are being tested to the limit.

(PAUSE): If you're picturing yet another male role model playing the part of the wise old mentor, here's a switcheroo.

The goddess Athena is known as the goddess of wisdom, courage, and heroic endeavors—and a cunning companion of heroes. The perfect superhero to have by your side, right?

She is watching Telemachus grow into a man and sees him now stepping off on his quest to find Dad. Recognizing that divine intervention might be necessary, Athena checks in with her father on Mount Olympus, Zeus, to receive permission to intervene. With a few caveats, permission is granted.

In one of the greatest shapeshifting maneuvers of all time, Athena assumes the appearance and role of Mentes, sets off to town to gather a crew of loyal men, and joins Odysseus' son on his years-long Hero's Journey.

The caveat that she must obey is to offer only guidance, insights, and assistance. She is never to fight Telemachus' battles, nor is she to tell him what he should do. Destiny must be earned.

After a very long and arduous road of trials, the young man is reunited with his dad, Odysseus. Father and son return to the island kingdom to overtake the infidels seeking the king's throne and Telemachus' birthright. Destiny is realized.

And they all live happily ever after.

For thousands of years now, men and women who follow in the footsteps of Mentes are known as mentors: crucial advisors and coaches during life's endless tests, tasks, and trials.

Destination – *Coaching and Mentoring*

As your journey is set to begin, wise counsel is your guide. Good coaching and mentoring are indispensable for a quest of this magnitude. In this chapter, you are introduced to the backstory of mentoring and its various modern incarnations.

Fellow Traveler – *Mentor*

Joining your entourage—and not a minute too soon—is your wise and insightful traveling companion, the mentor. Coaches and mentors are now, and should always be, key individuals in your life. They have traveled the path and illuminate your way toward life mastery.

The mentor shares experience, imparts wisdom, and conveys values. The mentor is the keeper of folklore, myths, and other life-shaping stories. Think of the wise old woman or man who has walked the path ahead of the hero and knows both the dangers and the secrets of a safe and fruitful passage. Preparing the hero for the tests, trials, and ordeals that lie ahead, the mentor implements training that provides essential lessons for the hero.

Mentors endow the hero with requisite knowledge and gifts that would take a lifetime to acquire. Your gift may be limited to knowledge and wisdom. For longer, more demanding journeys, you'll need something closer to divine intervention. This gift is one you need to earn. Most often, it is the exact thing you need in your darkest moment. Whatever the gift may be, the most important attribute you gain from it is confidence.

In meeting the mentor, you have access to wisdom that catapults you forward. The benefits of having a consummate teacher, a seasoned guide, and trusted confidant are essential when preparing for your calling. You receive indispensable advice, gain remarkable insight, and develop the confidence necessary for facing your challenges and fears.

Personal Guide – *Wisdom*

One quality that all of your personal assistants have in common is wisdom. That's why they're here. Your guide on this leg of the journey is the master of life lessons, the mentor. The strongest characteristic he possesses is wisdom. As your personal guide, wisdom shares freely—just know that it comes at a price.

Knowledge comes from learning; wisdom comes from experience. Much like the Hero's Journey itself, the process is one big continuum. We are learning beings, but without taking action and gaining experience, we have no shot at earning wisdom. It is the "been there, done that" syndrome complete with multiple mistakes, many bad judgments, and countless failures.

Greek philosophers spoke more of wisdom than any other topic. The Greek word *philosophia* means "love of wisdom." Practical wisdom enhances common sense and facilitates better decision-making. Meeting your mentor exposes you to the voice of experience and a depth of wisdom decades in the making.

> "The only true wisdom is in knowing you
> know nothing." ~ Socrates

FROM WOUNDS TO WISDOM

When you end up tripping over life, Oprah Winfrey advises, "Turn your wounds into wisdom." Unfortunately, my wound was believing I wasn't very smart. Turning that into wisdom seemed like a long shot.

I don't know if it was moving around so much as a kid and attending so many different schools (seven before the age of 12) or whether it was, in fact, that I had learning disabilities (as we now call them). It didn't make much difference; the end results were the same. Not smart. I was "less than" when it came to grades and measuring up to my peers.

What I learned instead was a work ethic—nose to the grindstone with a little elbow grease thrown in. *Doing* replaced *being*—that is, doing gratifying work instead of being smart. My wound set up an unreasonable assumption in the form of a shadow belief: "I'm not smart enough, so if I am going to make anything of myself, I have to *do* more than anyone else."

The role of the shadow is to destroy. On the surface, it seems nothing good can come from this, but it's quite the opposite. My shadow belief destroyed my self-worth, and as a result, I was forced to develop other skills and abilities such as doing more and being persistent. The revelation that came from this was that, in my experience, persistence outguns being smart every time.

So, how did I go from being a failure in school to teaching college and becoming the founder and dean of an educational institution with students from 37 countries?

Mentors.

When the hero is ready, the mentor appears.

I've had many mentors—some formal, most not. Growing up with my perceived intellectual disadvantage, I was attracted to people who were smarter than me (which left the field wide open). If I could emulate one good trait or learn from one bad mistake, I felt like I could earn a work-around. If I could collect enough "earnings," I could regain my self-worth.

GIFTS FROM THE MENTOR

Meeting the mentor is one of the most exciting stages of the journey. You understand and appreciate that you're not in this alone. Life is not a suicide mission, after all.

A good mentor doesn't need to be a wise old sage; they just need to be a little bit further down the path to carry the torch and guide you to the answers within. Mentors are all the good parts of humanity wrapped into one: trusted confidant, favored teacher, insightful friend, experienced guide, unwavering advocate, adept sparring partner, and enthusiastic cheerleader. Don't take this to mean that they won't be challenging or difficult at times. The good ones usually are.

Once you meet your mentor, life is never the same. Mentors most always appear just as you're about to leave the known ordinary world and enter the unknown special world (in our case, the transition from the conscious to the subconscious). This is when you need them the most as you're preparing for your quest.

The mentor's prime objective is to impart to the apprentice life lessons and life-shaping knowledge. The more options provided, the wiser a decision can be made by the one who lives with the consequences. Mentors have the awareness, know-how, and battlefield experience that would take a newbie years to gain, understand, and appreciate.

Mentors acknowledge what the apprentice desires and what they actually need. They have reflected on their successes and failures while on their journey. Mentors respect where the apprentice is on the path and why they need to be there. "If I knew then what I know now" moments are freely shared by the wise master and shrewdly accepted by a grateful protégé.

If commitment and competence are proven, the mentor may reward the hero with an essential "gift." The gift could be a treasure map, an antidote to the poison, a key to the vault, or some special magic needed for a successful quest. In many mythological stories, the hero is often required to pass a test to earn the gift.

After proving his abilities to Obi-Wan Kenobi, Luke Skywalker receives his father's lightsaber. Harry Potter gets past Fluffy, the three-headed guard dog, using a flute carved by Hagrid, his friend, protector, and a special type of mentor. The more traditional mentor in the *Harry Potter* series is Dumbledore. In the *Lord of the Rings* saga, this wise old man is Gandalf. Hitting the gift jackpot was Cinderella, who received a complete makeover. The fairy godmother turns a pumpkin into a coach, mice into horses, and the poor girl's rags into a beautiful gown. And let's not forget the all-important glass slippers. If it were not for her godmother, Cinderella would not have snagged her prince.

In *The Matrix*, Morpheus (Lawrence Fishburne) gives Neo (Keanu Reeves) a choice between a red pill and a blue pill. The red pill enables Neo to live in the real world. The blue pill allows him to remain in the Matrix to live and believe as he wishes. Ultimately, Neo chooses the pill that endows him with courage.

In *Dead Poets Society*, teacher John Keating (Robin Williams) dispenses to his students the timeless words of Horace, the leading Roman poet during the time of Augustus. Keating delights in sharing, "Carpe diem. Seize the day, boys. Make your lives extraordinary."

I had the opportunity to work with Tim Hill for about five years when he was the Director of Youth Markets at Walt Disney World. A goal of WDW is to exceed guest expectations. For Tim, it was a way of life. Exceeding expectations is who he is. I have no doubt this is who he was *before* he came to work for the Mouse, hence the attraction.

Tim's gift to me was as a role model. I doubt he'd ever believe he served as a mentor but he was exactly who and what I needed at that time in my life.

On the outside, Disney makes Herculean achievements look effortless. Behind the scenes, there's a company-wide obsession for undeniable quality and attention to detail, all sprinkled with a handful of pixie dust.

Tim's mentorship in what it takes to be the best became a meaningful piece of who I am today. Good mentors possess the magic to influence their apprentices in ways that are unexpected and with results that last a lifetime. Pretty good deal, if you ask me.

Mentors are a legitimate shortcut to the destination you desire. They offer "insider trading" that is not only legal but fully embraced by business executives, artists, politicians, athletes, and successful individuals of all types.

Ironically, not many people seek the advantage of a wise master. Since we are at the beginning of this journey, you should know that this is the only shortcut offered. You might as well take it. It's the only one you will get on this date with destiny.

When do you meet your mentor? Just like with students and teachers—when the hero is ready, the mentor appears.

COACHES, MENTORS, TEACHERS, AND GUIDES

In easily one of the most confusing times of her life, Dorothy's spinning house lands abruptly in the wonderful land of Oz. Her mentor, Glinda the Good Witch, magically appears at just the right moment with timely advice and a sparkling gift for her shoe closet.

Have you ever wondered why Glinda the Good Witch doesn't just give Dorothy the ruby slippers and have her click her heels to get back home?

For one, it would be a really short film. Second, Dorothy would not have learned a crucial life lesson that mentors are famous for providing: What you seek is already inside you.

During my tenure as the dean of Coach Training Alliance, we taught life coaches how to help clients find answers to their burning questions. Knowing where the answers are is easy. Finding them and digging them out is where the coach earns their fee.

You see, the coach doesn't have direct access to answers the client seeks. This is a dilemma, especially since the client is paying the coach for results. But coaches and mentors know the answers sought are within the client.

A coach helps extract the hidden code that has been within reach the entire time. It's unlikely that they'd be able to find and decrypt it on their own. A coach serves as an inner tour guide to the rugged terrain and unpredictable landscape of the subconscious—a cryptographer with a megaphone.

Of all the coaches, guides, teachers, and assistants on the Hero's Journey, the Mentor is my favorite. This is like having a technology geek in your ear telling you which way to turn, what corridor to run down, and when the bad guys will be coming around the corner. I could be a superhero, too, if I had that kind of advice streaming into my head in real time.

Well, you do—and "mentor" is the name. The essence of the mentor can embody itself in forms other than human. Whether it's an actual individual offering to take you under their wing, or a guardian angel on your shoulder commenting on what's ethical and what's not, you have the insights and advice you need to move forward.

The hero's conscience plays a pivotal mentor role if the hero has strayed from the appropriate or honorable path. Mentor is the wiser and nobler inner voice teaching us right from wrong. This form of the powerful archetype is representative of the most enlightened qualities present in our higher self.

Don't underestimate the little voice in your head. Sure it's great to have an Athena or Morpheus guiding you through the Matrix of life, but that little voice is right more often than it's wrong.

BEEN THERE, DONE THAT

Deep down, Will Hunting (who looks a lot like Matt Damon), needs to leave his small ordinary world and allow his potential (and relationships) to soar in the larger special world. Will's mentor in *Good Will Hunting* is psychologist Sean Maguire, played by the masterful Robin Williams (in the role of the mentor, once again). Maguire guides the angry and resistant hero in breaking down the barriers holding him back from hearing his inner voice—the voice that knows exactly what needs to happen.

As Maguire assures Will, "You'll have bad times, but it'll always wake you up to the good stuff you weren't paying attention to."

Mentors and coaches are valuable because, most often, they have been where you are, learned the hard lessons, and can now steer you on a better path. A good mentor doesn't need to be a wise old sage like Gandalf or Dumbledore; they just need to be a little bit further down the path than you are. It is said that the best teachers are those who have just learned what you need to know.

It wasn't that long ago that they were where you are now. Coaches and mentors know what questions you have, and they appreciate the obstacles you face. Experience has taught them hard-won lessons that they are anxious to share with you, minus the "hard-won" part.

To return victorious from the ordeal, the hero needs to become both physically and mentally stronger. Hard work and rigorous training are the hallmarks of many a great mentor. Ex-fighter and boxing trainer Mickey Goldmill pushes ambitious amateur Rocky Balboa to the limits. In a line adapted directly from the playbook of Zeus on Mount Olympus, Mickey tells Rocky, "You're gonna eat lightnin' and you're gonna crap thunder!"

"MUCH WISDOM, HE HAS"

No discussion on the mentor role would be complete without acknowledging the most well-known mentor in the galaxy, Yoda. Our syntax-challenged little friend offers many words of wisdom, he does. Those words may not come in a familiar order, but they are powerful, nonetheless.

Even though Yoda is small, balding, has big ears, and talks funny, he commands tremendous respect and admiration. The way Yoda speaks forces us to pay attention and heed his advice.

"Do. Or do not. There is no try."

When forced to give extra thought to the concept, our brains must reorder the words and reprocess the information. In less time than it takes you to read this sentence, your intelligence droid deduces that if you eliminate the word *try*, then you simply make up your mind to either do something or not. The mentor's point is made.

The linguistic challenge we face also has the side benefit of integrating a fundamental concept of pedagogy: repetition. As we listen to Yoda, we subconsciously customize the intention of what he says, so it makes more sense to us. By the time we're done processing this, the mentor's point is made several times over. Our active participation in the learning process increases our comprehension and retention exponentially.

The teachings and guidance given by the philosophers and mentors of the day weren't much different in ancient Greece from what they are today. Topics included health and diet, contemplation and meditation, and spirituality. Socrates characterized himself as "a midwife assisting the labor of the mind in bringing knowledge and wisdom to birth."

For those who have been mentored, mentorship becomes a tradition and honor. Socrates was Plato's teacher and inspiration. Plato taught Aristotle at the Academy for 20 years. Aristotle tutored Alexander the Great until the young king turned 16. The "disciples" of these Greek philosophers fanned out across the Roman Empire in an effort to enhance the lives of others and to "pay it forward." Think of it as life coaching in another era.

Incidentally, Alexander *was* great at creating one of the largest empires of the ancient world. Would he have been able to do this without the aid and influence of his mentor, Aristotle?

Mentoring is an age-old practice providing time-saving—and possibly life-saving—alternative routes on the path to destiny. The legacy that has cut a swath through time continues: Bach mentored Mozart, who mentored Beethoven. Renowned actor Laurence Olivier mentored Anthony Hopkins. Film director Martin Scorsese mentored Oliver Stone. Five-time Tour de France winner Eddy Merckx mentored Lance Armstrong. Music producer Dr. Dre mentored Eminem.

It's not necessary to be mentored by someone in a similar role or profession, but these relationships are most easily recognized. In fact, the mentor doesn't even need to be alive to strongly influence the hero and greatly impact the world.

TOGA PARTY

Hollywood is fond of creating mentor characters that audiences can easily define. Many end up wearing the obligatory robe presumably handed down from Greek philosophers. In the ordinary world, don't expect your choice of mentors to be wearing long, flowing, hooded robes (although that *does* sound cool). Hollywood has the market cornered on this wardrobe.

In real life, the movie and television business is rich with mentor/protégé relationships: Audrey Hepburn mentored Elizabeth Taylor. Gary Cooper mentored Kirk Douglas, who then mentored his son, Michael. Barbara Walters mentored Oprah Winfrey. In an interview, Winfrey told Walters, "Had there not been you, there never would have been me."

The list and the apprenticeships continue, and not just in the film and entertainment business.

Founding Father George Mason was a mentor to Thomas Jefferson. Ralph Waldo Emerson mentored fellow writer Henry David Thoreau. American economist and professional investor Benjamin Graham mentored Warren Buffet, who went on to mentor Bill Gates. Google founders Larry Page and Sergey Brin mentored Marissa Mayer, who went on to become CEO of Yahoo!. Semiconductor pioneer Andy Grove mentored Steve Jobs, who then mentored Mark Zuckerberg.

Do you see a pattern here? Highly successful people recognize they didn't make it to the top by themselves. They mentor promising young apprentices who attain their own level of success, in their own way. Those new masters go on to mentor other promising young apprentices. Doesn't it make you want to step in line and pick out a great mentor?

In all walks of life, there are mentor/apprentice, mentor/protégé, and coach/client relationships. These respected relationships are quickening the learning curve, bypassing game-changing obstacles, and revealing the shortest distance from where you are now to where you want to be.

If you believe having a coach or mentor is just for the big shots, think again. Hundreds of thousands of people participate in this time-honored tradition. Most likely, you're looking up to some of them without even realizing the totally accessible edge they possess.

Everyone suffers through tough times, endures distressing childhoods, and encounters formidable obstacles throughout their life. (Did you really think you had the market cornered on this?) No matter where you've come from or where you are right now, you can also enjoy the gifts and good fortune of coaching and mentoring.

Indra Nooyi credits mentoring for helping her break glass ceilings in her career. Born in Chennai, India, in 1955, Nooyi now directs PepsiCo's global strategy and is consistently ranked among the World's Most Powerful Women. What a Hero's Journey it must have been for her—from growing up as a little girl in India to becoming the chairperson and CEO of the second-largest food and beverage business in the world, a position she's held for more than a decade. "Coaches or mentors are very important," says Nooyi, "If I hadn't had mentors, I wouldn't be here today. I'm a product of great mentoring . . . great coaching."

Who is your coach? Who do you look to as a mentor? Nobody successfully navigates the Hero's Journey by themselves. Do you think the people mentioned above just got lucky in their success, or did they have help?

Wait, I get it. You've been a loner/outcast all your life. This kind of relationship doesn't sound like it's going to work for you. Guess what? There's a successful loner/outcast mentor who has been where you are and felt the same way you feel now. Wouldn't it be incredible to have a conversation with them?

A good coach or mentor helps guide you to your purpose and the meaning that brings to your life. Heady stuff, for sure, but without this self-knowledge, you won't have much of a lead character in the story of your life.

Find yourself a coach or mentor (toga optional). Become the apprentice of your best life. When push comes to shove, and you're all by yourself, listen to your inner coach, a voice that is always with you and knows what you want and what's best for you.

One doesn't become a hero overnight. Becoming the hero of your life requires an apprenticeship in the art and science of self-discovery. Step up and lean into your place in line. As an apprentice, you'll enjoy a major shortcut to the life you desire. Your turn as mentor to someone else on their own Hero's Journey will be even more rewarding.

EXPLORING YOUR ROLE

Mentors provide a legitimate shortcut to the destination you desire. They have the awareness, know-how, and experience embraced by successful individuals of all types.

- When the hero is ready, the mentor appears.
- Mentors impart life-shaping knowledge.
- Learn from experience—preferably someone else's.
- Having a coach or mentor is not just for the big shots.
- Mentoring is a "pay it forward" activity.

If you are ready for your mentor and one has not appeared, look closer. Seek them out. Connecting with a mentor is your job, not theirs. Not sure where to start? Hire a coach.

It will be great to finally get some professional help (like your friends are always telling you). Help and guidance that is beneficial and *all about you*!

Even if you don't have the benefit of a personal coach or mentor, pay attention to your inner dialogue. It's trying desperately to tell you something, and frankly, no one else is listening.

Following your heart, your bliss, and your dreams doesn't have to be needlessly complicated, demanding, or painful. A good coach or mentor will have you negotiating your destiny from a position of power.

In the words of a master mentor, "Nothing more will I teach you today."

ᚙ Self-Discovery ᚙ

1. When you were growing up, who did you look to for guidance and direction?
2. Are there others who acted—directly or indirectly— as your teacher or coach?
3. How would your life be different had you never met these individuals?
4. How could your life be different now if you did have a coach or mentor?

CHAPTER 8

LEAP OF FAITH

It takes courage to grow up and become
who you really are. ~ E.E. Cummings

Butch:	We'll jump!
	The raging stream below is fifty feet down and moving fast.
Sundance:	Like hell we will.
Butch:	No, it'll be okay—if the water's deep enough and we don't get squished—they'll never follow us.
Sundance:	How do you know?
Butch:	Would you make a jump like that if you didn't have to?

Sundance: I have to and I'm not gonna.

Butch: Well, we got to otherwise we're dead. They're just gonna have to go back down the way they come.

Sundance: Just one clear shot that's all I want.

Butch: Come on.

Sundance: No

Butch: We got to.

Sundance: Nope. Get away from me.

Butch: Why?

Sundance: I wanna fight 'em.

Butch: They'll kill us.

Sundance: Maybe.

Butch: You wanna die?

Sundance: Do you? *(motioning toward the raging stream below)*

Butch: Alright, I'll jump first.

Sundance: Nope.

Butch: Then you jump first.

Sundance: No, I said.

Butch: What's the matter with you?

Sundance: I CAN'T SWIM!

Butch starts to roar while Sundance is angry and embarrassed.

Butch: Are you crazy? The fall'll probably kill you.

The boys move to the edge of the path and make a leap of faith. Falling through the twilight they drop abruptly—yet safely—into the waters below.

This scene is from the Academy Award–winning script for the 1969 film *Butch Cassidy and the Sundance Kid*, written by William Goldman (*The Princess Bride, All the President's Men*).

The super posse chasing Butch and Sundance has our heroes cornered with no way out. There is nothing left to do except to muster the courage and make the leap.

Who can't identify with this? We've all been in similar situations. Maybe not as physically demanding, dangerous, or dire, but every bit as mentally perplexing and emotionally taxing. Be forewarned, my hero, for you are arriving at such a standoff on *your* adventure. Prepare yourself to make a leap of faith. You may not want to look down, but do look back at an ordinary world you are destined to change.

Destination – *Purpose and Passion*

Your objective on this leg of the journey is to accurately define and refine your purpose and passion. Your skills, talents, and abilities fuse together, revealing the internal engine that powers your endowments. Once you have a solid handle on these, your potential grows exponentially.

Fellow Traveler – *Allies*

Friends, allies, and buddies come to your aid in a crisis and help activate the unused or unexpressed parts of your personality. Sometimes, just having someone to talk with forces you to verbalize what had only been a thought or idea.

As in the ordinary world, allies are earned. Friends, buddies, and sidekicks assist and comfort us through the massive changes we encounter. We want to win as many allies as possible to support us through the transitions and transformations.

Buddy movies are a Hollywood staple: Danny Glover and Mel Gibson in the *Lethal Weapon* series; Geena Davis and Susan Sarandon in *Thelma & Louise*; Will Smith and Tommy Lee Jones in *Men in Black*; and, of course, Paul Newman and Robert Redford in *Butch Cassidy and the Sundance Kid* and *The Sting*. It's reassuring and affirming to have a friend along to share the experience—all of it, both the triumphs and the defeats.

Allies unite for mutual benefit or to attain a common goal. Friends wouldn't be friends for long if the hero only used them for selfish purposes. Butch needs Sundance, Thelma needs Louise, Murtaugh needs Riggs, and vice versa.

Personal Guide – *Courage*

Courage is with you now to help you act in spite of fear. You leave the ordinary world behind and enter a special world promising transformation and rewards. With Courage as your guide, you learn there is much you need not fear if you're willing to take the leap.

When the ancient Greek philosophers talked about courage, it was in reference to one's character on the battlefield. Aristotle believed the virtue of bravery empowered Greek soldiers to manage their fears, enabling them to fight the battle courageously.

Similarly, the doubts and fears we face on our inner journey require moral courage. We must be willing and able to act on our ethical beliefs and values, and to stand on principle.

Doing the right thing sometimes entails going against popular opinion, being shamed by peers, or even suffering a personal loss. Being able to "walk your talk" down this path comes at a price. When you stand up for what's right, you may be standing alone.

The good news is, you can gain the courage of your convictions with practice. At this level, it's like being thrown in the deep end to learn how to swim. You must be courageous to possess courage. You must take action in spite of your fears, or you will drown. The next time in the water may still be a little scary, but you've acquired an ounce of bravery—and it looks good on you. Pretty soon, summoning courage is no longer necessary—your courageous character prevails.

> "You can choose courage or you can choose comfort but you cannot choose both." ~ Brené Brown

PUSHING THROUGH THE FEAR

The leap taken by Butch and Sundance is both literal and metaphorical. From here, they escape into the special world of South America, where everything is different, including the language. These two allies are stronger together than they would be individually. The allies you meet on your path offer a shoulder to lean on, lend you an ear, and watch your back. Some will even jump off of a cliff with you.

Leaps of faith come in all shapes and sizes. The leap you'll need to make is custom-fit just for you, based on what you need to learn and where you plan on heading. Here's another film moment that requires the hero to make a leap of faith, but in a very different way from Butch and Sundance.

Harry is encouraged to get moving by his ally and mentor, Hagrid. The half-giant, half-human from Hogwarts has given Harry Potter his golden ticket: the one that's going to take him on the train bound for a strange and special world. It's leaving in ten minutes, so he must make haste.

Harry has a very particular platform from which he is supposed to board the train. He looks everywhere between platforms nine and ten but can't find his platform. He spots a trainmaster and asks where he might find Platform 9 ¾. "9 ¾?" The trainmaster doesn't look pleased. "Think you're being funny, do ya?" And he walks off.

A woman named Mrs. Weasley walks by with her family. "Come on," she says, "Platform 9 ¾ this way." One of the boys runs toward the brick wall and disappears right into it. Harry can't believe his eyes. Then two more of the boys run through the wall. Harry looks to the woman, who tells him, "All you've got to do is walk straight at the wall between platforms nine and ten. Best do it at a bit of a run if you're nervous."

It's a quite-literal leap of faith, but Harry takes a deep breath, runs at the wall, shuts his eyes, and magically appears on the other side. Waiting for him is a red train whose whistle is blowing for the departure from Platform 9 ¾ to the Hogwarts School of Witchcraft and Wizardry.

All leaps of faith look different, feel different, and are different. You can't prepare yourself for what your challenge will be. It will come to you on its own, often more quickly than not.

Your significant other gets an amazing job offer on the other side of the country. Your quality of life "should" skyrocket. But you'll have to leave your friends and family, and everything you currently find comfortable. Your S.O. is your ally and has always been there for you. Will you take the leap?

The leap of faith is where most people chicken out on the Hero's Journey. The leap requires resolute courage and lands those who attempt it squarely outside of their comfort zone. Resistance to change runs high. Refusing the call is easy. That is, it *was* easy until you became aware. The awareness stage of the journey has a way of shedding light on the immutable truth.

You come to a point in your inner life where what you once thought was of prime importance (your looks, your career, your possessions) somehow slips down the rankings. Letting it go means losing a significant part of your identity. Keeping it stunts your growth. Life might be better. Or not. Finding out requires a leap of faith.

The choice belongs to the hero in the arena—the one who has answered the call, is striving valiantly, and daring greatly, as Teddy Roosevelt would say.

How many calls have you refused? How many of those do you wish you could do over? If you get a second chance, where will you find the strength, determination, and power to push through the wall?

PASSION REVEALS POWER

Uncovering your power begins with recognizing your passions and landing on your purpose. According to the Gallup-Healthways Global Well-Being Index, only 9% of adults globally are thriving when it comes to their sense of purpose, making it the most neglected category of well-being.

Becoming aware of your purpose doesn't usually come in a "light bulb" moment. Pieces of purpose may come to you in this way, but what normally transpires is a slow burn that ignites a process of becoming.

The first stage of awareness is dropping all the preconceived notions of what you think your purpose is, what you've been encouraged it should be, or what those close to you wish it could be. "If you want to discover your true purpose in life," advises personal-development expert Steve Paulina, "You must first empty your mind of all the false purposes you've been taught, including the idea that you may have no purpose at all."

Taking care of your family, putting food on the table, and being a good person is not your specific purpose. Yes, these are worthy objectives, but they could apply to just about anyone. What is *your* purpose? Where is your power buried? What is unique about you that stands out and makes a difference? What do you do better than anyone else you know?

Dig deep enough and I promise you're going to unearth your purpose, and in so doing, uncover your power. When you're "on," when you're in the zone, when things are flowing effortlessly for you, you're in your power spot. You're passionate about what you're doing. You find it fulfilling and rewarding. Chances are, you're helping others thrive in the process. Everybody wins; everybody benefits. This is real power.

Often, purpose and passion are so entwined, they can almost seem to be one. If you had to untangle them, you might observe this distinction: Purpose is the reason you're on this journey. Passion is the torch that lights your way. Follow your passions and you'll run smack into your purpose.

If that analogy doesn't quite work for you, look at it this way: When you're driving yourself to improve your talents, skills, and abilities, it's purpose that's behind the wheel. Where's passion? That's your foot on the accelerator.

In the interest of presenting a differing point of view, here's Mike Rowe, host of the television show *Dirty Jobs*: "Don't follow your passions; bring them with you." Some people following their passions are still waiting tables while waiting for their big break. And while persistence is key to surviving and thriving, maybe there's a better way to reach the top.

"Do something you're good at and figure out a way to love it," Rowe says. A slogan like that will never make it onto a success poster with a photo of a guy standing on top of a mountain. But you're more likely to climb your metaphorical Everest—being good at what you do and loving it—than you would following a passion that may be better suited as a hobby (or a part-time job).

Life on Purpose author Brad Swift maintains that life purpose is not about something you do, some role you play, or some job you have. The things we do aren't what define our purpose but are expressions of our purpose. Our purpose isn't what we do; it is what shapes what we do. Purpose is not in the *what* but the *why*. It's not in the *doing* but in the *being*.

UNCOVERING YOUR POWER

We are each born with the capacity to fulfill a life purpose. We were born to flourish. Our passions, often unbeknownst to us, emanate from our life purpose and vice-versa. It is an infinite loop of fire for the soul. The relationship between purpose and passion won't be fully appreciated until we come full circle in our search for destiny. The most significant action we can take now is to recognize, acknowledge, and honor our purpose and pursue it with unbridled passion.

When you are truly on purpose, the people, resources, and opportunities you need naturally gravitate toward you. Jack Canfield, author of *The Success Principles*, emphasizes, "Be clear why you're here." Without a purpose, it's easy to get sidetracked on your life's journey.

Start with possibility thinking—that is, not your current limitations, but what is possible. You won't nail your life's purpose in 10–20 minutes. Even if you manage to isolate 30–40 minutes of uninterrupted alone time, it still may not crystalize. However, you'll be closer and might even discard surface-level notions, pat answers, and other people's expectations. This is your trip, so enjoy the momentary solitude. Gradually, with consistent self-examination and honest appraisal, you'll come closer to a meaningful purpose statement.

On some level, you already know the reason you are the hero of your myth. Why did you answer the call? What is so special about you? What are your gifts? Like the mythical heroes on Mount Olympus, you, too, have a superpower. What is it? Come up with the answers to these questions and you are incredibly close to defining your true purpose.

What are you better at than anyone you know?

Purpose reveals itself in dreams, desires, and wishes. (They may not get you where you want to go, but chances are you're not going to end up where you think you will, anyway.) What did you dream as a kid? What are your dreams now? What is your default daydream? Which dream have you had the longest?

Dream big, but don't get locked in. Be open and hold space for something you hadn't planned to discover. As *The Lovely Bones* author Alice Sebold points out, "Sometimes the dreams that come true are the dreams you never even knew you had."

Joseph Campbell said, "Myths, so to say, are public dreams; dreams are private myths." (Campbell, 1972) What is the private story you most want to read? What do you want your myth to be? What story will you write?

Stories influence minds and determine fates. We see it all the time on television and in the movies. What little kid doesn't emulate their favorite superhero? What adult doesn't secretly wish they were living the life they see on the screen? It's so rewarding to see other people overcoming all odds and persevering to save the world (and get the girl/guy). In a quiet sort of way, stories inspire us to believe we just might be able to do the same thing—someday.

One hiding place to find our purpose/passion is in something we already possess: innate ability. We may not recognize that we have it, so it doesn't immediately come to mind. That's because, when you use your natural abilities, there's nothing to it—so it's easy to think everybody can do it. They can't.

My friend Robert W. Smith is a musical genius. The word "genius" gets thrown around a lot, but this guy is the real deal. Not only does he have perfect pitch (the innate ability to hear a note and be able to tell you it's an F sharp, for example) he also writes full music scores in his head before transferring them to a format other people can read. He does all of this on an airplane or on a beach without the aid of a piano or musical keyboard of any kind. He's a freak (in a good way). He told me that when he was growing up, he didn't think anything of it because it was easy for him to do. For the longest time, he thought *everybody* could do it.

And so it is with many innate talents and abilities.

You possess a unique combination of skills, talents, and abilities that make you perfect to play the hero. Everything you need to figure out, everything you must do, everything you need to be, is waiting to be discovered. The answers come from your own inner hero. For your part (the conscious part), the mandate is uncovering your power.

For me—someone who barely made it through high-school English—my passion is crafting words. Go figure. It took me the better part of my life to uncover my purpose because I didn't do well in school and didn't think I was smart. Ironically, learning and teaching are two of my gifts. (Who says the universe doesn't have a sense of humor?)

What I'm better at than anyone I know is distilling knowledge. I evaluate, aggregate, coalesce, systematize, and clarify information for greater understanding. I pull together, assemble, and condense knowledge for heightened awareness, comprehension, and enlightenment. From this collection of attributes, I created a purpose statement that is the headline of my master plan.

On this unpredictable journey, I've tripped over my dreams, fallen into my purpose, and landed on my passion.

My purpose is helping people discover their life's path by charting new adventures in personal growth and lifelong learning.

It might sound a little corny, but it works for me. What works for you should be equally as corny in a uniquely you sort of way. Your purpose statement becomes an integral part of your Map of Self-Discovery.

PROOF OF PURPOSE

Now that we've been encouraged to emulate our screen heroes and follow our dreams, here's the downside: Dreams engender feelings. Feelings arouse passion. Passion reveals purpose.

So far, so good.

Passion drives your feelings and purpose, and is the profound reason for your existence. But following your dreams, as we're so often told to do, can be a setup for failure. Grand dreams require planning, resources, sustained effort, and time. It's *time* that usually trips up even the best of heroes. Who can sustain genuine commitment over a silly "positive thinking" dream or the inspiration from a special-effects movie?

In dreams and movies, we rarely get to see what it takes to get to the point of the payoff. There's only so much filmmakers can show in under two hours, and preparation is mundane. That's what gets cut from the movie or not even shot in the first place.

In real life, we're looking at years of training, along with sacrifice and unrelenting resistance from many unseen forces. Olympic athletes train and dedicate themselves for four years to participate in an event that is measured in minutes and seconds. Commitment is the tip of the iceberg when it comes to making big dreams come true.

A dedicated life purpose is a gift and something we must prove worthy of. Just as we earn the gift from the mentor, we must provide proof of commitment to our purpose. A life purpose is nothing more than words in a journal unless we leap off the page and put action to our words.

When we genuinely land on our purpose, taking action is not an issue. The proof of our purpose comes when we experience inspiration, awakening, and aliveness. We eagerly embrace the commitment to our purpose because it feels right, it's sustainable, and we can't wait to go after it.

"When you are inspired by some great purpose, some extraordinary project, all your thoughts break their bonds: Your mind transcends limitations, your consciousness expands in every direction, and you find yourself in a new, great, and wonderful world. Dormant forces, faculties, and talents become alive, and you discover yourself to be a greater person by far than you ever dreamed yourself to be." These words of wisdom date back to 150 BC and were written by the Indian sage Patañjali, compiler of the *Yoga Sūtras*.

WORK IN PROGRESS

No one leaps into this kind of battle without a plan. There's too much at stake. We've barely started our journey, and there are so many aspects and intricacies to consider. The best place to start is at the center and work our way out.

There are numerous interconnected components that come together to form a master plan for life: a purpose statement, core values, guiding principle, personal mission, core competencies, career anchors, and a HUB statement. This is your Hottest Undeniable Benefit from which everything else emanates.

The statement you craft is a concise description of who you want to serve, the compelling challenges they face, and why your unique talents and abilities benefit them. Questions are the spokes that lead to the HUB.

- Who are you at the core?
- What is the center of your being?
- What distinguishes you from your friends and colleagues?
- Who are you when things are going well and life is good?
- What are you doing when you find yourself totally engaged and time flies?

The answers to these questions help you explore the heart and soul of who you are. The HUB leads directly to the chamber where your purpose is waiting to be discovered.

As part of my inner work, I developed a "Life Well Lived Master Plan." It includes all the components mentioned above. I haven't shared this with too many people, but since I've already opened the door, here's a peek inside my HUB statement. My Hottest Undeniable Benefit is that I think of myself as a triple threat: a Writer-Producer-Photographer. I create dynamic stories for people discovering their purpose and passion, by using engaging content, visual metaphors, and captured moments.

Keep in mind that you needn't be humble when you write this for yourself. No one else needs to see it. For me, it feels somewhat awkward to share what comes off as such a boastful statement, but I want you to see how it works.

All of the components of my master plan move and morph, and have a life all their own. Some pieces stick and have been around for years; others, for decades. Still other parts change as needed. Even though your plan is to "commit" to your purpose, be open to the idea that it may end up being very different from what you first envision.

Long-term goals, your personal mission, the purpose statement, etc., are anything but static. They are impossibly impermanent. Your aim here is not to land on the one thing you will do for the rest of your life. Your intention is simply to define a jumping-off point from which you can alter, adjust, and transform the hero within. This is your leap of faith.

I've been writing my master plan for decades now. For the first few years, I made small changes, minor adjustments, and various tweaks. Months or years down the road, I'd find myself making further modifications and improvements. It wasn't until recently that I realized my master plan is under constant revision. I never stopped tweaking it—and rightly so. We are all a work in progress (some more than others), and our ever-changing plan is a reflection of this.

For example, ten years ago my HUB looked very different from the one you just read. Life happens, circumstances change, and the unexpected fork in the road triggers reassessments. Expect to be surprised (both pleasantly and otherwise) that your life isn't turning out as you had designed in your master plan.

Disclaimer: In the long run, the master plan isn't going to be worth the paper it's written on. Dreams evolve, plans shift, and pivots are made. So, why sacrifice the brain cells to develop a plan in the first place?

PLANNING IS EVERYTHING

On June 6, 1944, more than 160,000 troops, 5,000 ships, and 13,000 aircraft descended on the beaches of Normandy, France, during World War II. Allied forces consisting of British, American, and Canadian military persevered through bad weather, thousands of casualties, and significant enemy resistance.

That day on Omaha Beach in German-occupied France, very little went as planned. Rough seas and strong currents swamped many landing crafts, and the ones that did make it were way off course and bunched up in disorganized chaos. Tanks and other heavy equipment sank before making it to the beach. The pre-landing air assault intended to take out enemy artillery and strongholds was delayed by weather. When the bombers finally arrived, Allied forces were nearing the target area. To avoid hitting them, the bombs were dropped late, consequently missing the intended enemy targets. The landing troops that survived long enough to make it to the beach found themselves under heavy fire and suffering massive casualties.

Commanding General and future U.S. President Dwight D. Eisenhower was asked how the plan was working. He replied, "Plans are nothing. Planning is everything."

Eisenhower makes an important distinction here—a good one to keep in mind. Regardless of how psychic a character you may be, life is not going to happen the way you plan it.

The fact that you have a plan, though, gives you a base from which to work. With a plan, you can now augment, modify, and adapt to changing conditions and tactical advantages.

Some people get discouraged when their plans don't come together. They use this as an excuse to quit. "Well, at least I gave it my best."

Reality check: Plans rarely deliver the desired results. The real work begins when the plan *doesn't* come together. That's where the hero's persistence and tenacity step up to revise and course-correct.

Can you imagine not having a plan for the Normandy Invasion on D-Day? Likewise, can you imagine not having a plan for the far-reaching quest upon which you have embarked?

EXPLORING YOUR ROLE

This is your leap of faith. An exhilarating jump from the ordinary world to the special world, from the conscious to the unconscious, from merely living on the surface of life to immersing yourself in the depths of a life well lived.

Your courage is tested. Bravely face the tests and trials that bring new possibilities and positive experiences to yourself and others. This is the hero's quest.

You aren't alone. Allies are awaiting your arrival and are set to tame and temper the gusty winds and raging waters. An ally can be a protector, a confidant, a cheerleader, or a sparring partner.

The finest allies to have are those who bring out the best in you—or help you get rid of the worst. Allies help activate the unused or unexpressed parts of the hero's personality. Sometimes, just having someone to talk with forces the hero to verbalize what had only been a thought or idea lying captive in a resolute mind.

Purpose and passion are yours to define and refine. Change is in the air.

- Act in spite of fear.
- Take responsibility—it's where your powers live.
- Ask yourself the fundamental question: What are you better at than anyone you know?

Begin pulling notes and ideas together to start your master plan. It's a good jumping off-point when supplemented with the understanding that plans change. All the same, writing them down makes them real and helps you arrive at the core of your being.

⚞ Self-Discovery ⚟

1. What dreams do you have—day or night—that are revealing your purpose?
2. What are your hidden gifts and talents? What is your superpower?
3. Is there something in which you excel, that you may not recognize because you're so close to it?
4. What's your plan? If you're not writing any of this down your ideas could be evaporating.

"I'd be happy to follow my passion, if I only knew what it was."

Discover your purpose at:
willcraig.com/gifts

CHAPTER 9

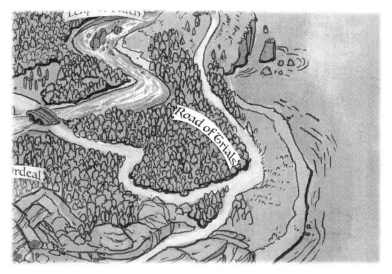

ROAD OF TRIALS

Before you begin the journey, you own the journey.
Once you have begun, the journey owns you.
~ Old Proverb

Near the beginning of the 1977 movie *Star Wars*, our soon-to-be hero, Luke Skywalker (Mark Hamill), meets his mentor, Obi-Wan Kenobi (Alec Guinness). Along with R2D2 and C3PO, they're on their way to find the smuggler Han Solo in the city of Mos Eisley. Soon after arriving in the city, they are stopped by a half-dozen Imperial 117tormtroopers asking for identification. Luke thinks they're doomed until his mentor pulls a Jedi mind trick.

117

LIVING THE HERO'S JOURNEY

Obi-Wan:	These aren't the droids you're looking for.
Stormtrooper:	These aren't the droids we're looking for.
Obi-Wan:	He can go about his business.
Stormtrooper:	You can go about your business.
Obi-Wan:	Move along.
Stormtrooper:	Move along . . . move along.

Our guys finally locate the small-time smuggler in the cantina. Han Solo finally agrees to take his new passengers to the planet Alderaan and prepares the *Millennium Falcon*, the fastest ship in the galaxy. A hasty exit is forced by an attacking garrison of stormtroopers looking for a couple of droids (nobody said Jedi mind tricks last forever). After blasting their way out of Mos Eisley, the *Falcon* and crew run into a couple of Star Destroyers and are nearly captured before pulling out all the stops and making the jump to lightspeed.

For Luke Skywalker, this is the hero's leap of faith. He has left the ordinary world of his farm-boy existence and is entering the special world of Jedi warriors and the Force.

So begins Luke's road of trials.

Destination – *Fate and Fortune*

It helps to possess an understanding of where our journey might take us. Before we learn our fate, we must earn our fortune. In this case, it's not so much about possessing the riches of fortune but in the good fortune of knowing thyself

Fellow Traveler – *Threshold Guardian*

The role of the threshold guardian is to test. This gatekeeper challenges our doubts and fears. Our persistence and perseverance are on trial. Are we worthy of the fortune we seek?

The threshold is a gateway to the special world where the hero seizes the reward of transformation and renewal. As you might imagine, such an important entry point does not go unprotected. The threshold guardian prevents the unworthy from entering this zone of magnified power. The hero must be ready, willing, and able to accept this power and deploy it to its highest and best use. The hero's resolve is thoroughly tested in the pursuit of destiny. If it is not the hero's time to make this journey, the guardian compels the hero to turn back until he or she evolves, matures, and musters the courage of their convictions.

The primary function of the threshold guardian is to prove that the hero is capable. In mythology, this is accomplished through a series of tests and trials. The hero must joust with a villain, clash with a titan, or battle enemy forces with incredible strength and firepower. And this is just the outward journey.

In defeating those forces and rising victorious in the face of adversity, the hero grows immeasurably. Overcoming the threshold guardian gives the hero greater strength, more confidence, and increased wisdom. The hero is better for the encounter. It becomes easier to see this archetype as an ally than solely as an enemy. The threshold guardian provides the proving grounds for a new and improved hero.

These guardians take many forms and are easily spotted because they are the person or the thing keeping us from obtaining who or what we want. Indiana Jones experienced a threshold guardian in the form of a gigantic boulder rolling after him in the opening scene of *Raiders of the Lost Ark*. Influential business people often have assistants who act as gatekeepers restricting access to these very busy professionals. Make it through the "gauntlet" and you're one step closer to getting what you want.

Personal Guide – *Integrity*

The guide of integrity is our closest companion and confidant for this segment. Adversity doesn't build character; it reveals it. The temptation to disregard our moral compass will be strong. It is crucial to walk our talk and live our values, or be compelled to walk this road again.

The word *integrity* originates from the Latin *integer*, meaning "whole" or "complete." Integrity involves acting consistently within the framework of expectations, actions, and outcomes. Heroes possess integrity when they are congruent with their values, operate within their belief system, and abide by their principles. In so doing, they experience an inner sense of wholeness—and along with it, a contentment with having walked their talk. That comfort is the warmth of the guide of integrity who has shared each step.

You know when you're honest and truthful. You also feel the lack of integrity when you're not sincere or honorable. Two things inhibit the good intention of walking your talk: fear and motivation. No doubt, you sense by now that you will face your fears along the path you have chosen. As with other times in your life, when you face those fears, there may be a tendency to keep talking but stop moving. Look to your guides for motivation. They are your accountability partners. When you hold yourself accountable, you walk hand in hand with your guides and find the journey less burdensome and more enlightening

> "Integrity is doing the right thing, even when no one is watching." ~ C.S. Lewis

THE ROAD AHEAD

Taking a quick look at the Map of Self-Discovery, awareness was just the beginning of our journey. Thrill though it may have been, the adventure has just begun.

Awareness	Call to Adventure
	Meeting the Mentor
	Leap of Faith
Change	Road of Trials
	The Ordeal
	Transformation
Renewal	Endowment
	Life Mastery

121

We have left the awareness stage and are heading directly into the choppy waters of change. For better or worse, the change stage is the most arduous, and at the same time, most beneficial and rewarding.

What is the most important thing we learn in our state of heightened awareness? Our "why."

It was German philosopher and Greek scholar Friedrich Nietzsche who said, "He who has a why to live can bear almost any how." Our why is our purpose. The how is uncovered on the road of trials.

The road of trials is a metaphor for the training and testing of the hero. The only judge at these trials is you. This is where you develop the skills, abilities, and experience necessary to fulfill your destiny. Weaknesses are addressed, performance is improved, and confidence is gained.

Lessons learned on the road prepare us for the final exam in the next chapter: the ordeal.

HEROISM EXPECTED

For our friends in the *Millennium Falcon*, it was a leap to lightspeed that brought them to a special world. In the movies, running off into battle is glamorous and compelling—especially if you're making the jump to hyperspace. The truth is, when you're the one with boots on the ground, it's a whole different story. How you perform, what you learn, and how you conduct yourself will determine your fate and influence your destiny.

Just because you now have a purpose statement doesn't mean it will be smooth sailing. Doubt, second guessing, and fear of failure will have their day on your road of trials. Having a purpose, however, enables you to focus your future and to choose your battles wisely. There will be many from which to select.

Yes, life is a struggle. Living the Hero's Journey is an even bigger challenge. Who said it was going to be easy? The modern media tries to convince us that we should be happy and our lives joyous. We deserve it, after all. Anyone who buys this new car, or shops at this store, or drinks this product will be happy and fulfilled. We're bombarded daily with these messages. When we first hear them, we know they're exaggerated and unrealistic claims. After many years of repetition, part of us begins to believe the hype, while the other part already feels entitled to be happy and fulfilled.

The expectation of living the "good life" replaces the struggle and strife that is part of our daily existence. This notion is one of the downsides of social conditioning and only replicates unhappiness and lack of fulfillment.

What's needed is courage and heroism. How much better off would we be if everyone took themselves on, endured the transformation, and made the world a better place?

Sitting back waiting for our entitlements is robbing us of a life well lived. "To radically advance our lives, we will no doubt endure real struggle," writes Brendon Burchard, author of *The Motivation Manifesto*. "We mustn't complain about it or fail to anticipate it."

The struggle, hardship, and perseverance give us the power to direct our destiny. Why would we give that away in hopes of getting something for nothing, which we know isn't coming?

From where do this courage and heroism emanate? Purpose and passion. These two potions mixed in the proper proportions brew a potent blend. Unfortunately, the Hero's Brew is not available at Starbucks—yet.

Think about when you go to the movies. Do you want to see a documentary film where the main character is smart, makes all the right moves, and becomes a likable leader in his community? Or do you want to see an action-adventure flick where the down-and-out hero perseveres through countless hardships, beats the odds, and emerges victorious while saving the world?

If you said yes to the latter, why is it that the struggles we're ready to take on and the hardships we're willing to endure involve appearing to be smart, wanting to make all the right moves, and being liked by everyone?

RITES OF PASSAGE

Rites of passage are important acts, rituals, or ceremonies marking the passage of an individual or community from one stage of life to another. The religious rituals of baptism, confirmation, and ordination are rites of passage. Marriage is another rite of passage. Funerals are a rite of passage, albeit the last rite.

In many cultures, coming of age is recognized as a rite of passage. In parts of Central and South America, the *quinceañeara* is celebrated by young girls when they turn 15 years old. In Kenya and Tanzania, the Maasai tribe perform initiations for young boys joining the "warrior class" of manhood. The bar and bat mitzvahs for Jewish boys and girls are a coming-of-age tradition closer to home.

The vision quest sends young men to fend for themselves in an attempt to achieve the vision of a future guardian spirit that also becomes the vision to support the entire community. The quest is common among the Native American Plains tribes. Young men head off into the wild for several days of fasting, exposure to the elements, and lessons in self-reliance as they prepare to enter adulthood.

In most rites, pain, sacrifice, loss, and isolation are all part of the ritual. An initial stage of departure divorces the individual from the familiar. In the initiation phase, the old identity is destroyed and replaced with a newer self. The return marks a reintegration into society in a new role.

In modern society, formal rites of passage have lessened in popularity, although we all travel the road of trials, ready or not. Attempting to avoid the pain and sacrifice only delays growth and maturity.

The helicopter parent who wants to make sure their child never experiences anything bad unwittingly takes away the building blocks of a future life well lived. At what point will those children learn life lessons and the consequences of their actions? Will they prepare for the real world, or will they grow up feeling entitled to a pain-free existence?

We spend so much time attempting to avoid the pain and anguish of growth that we deny ourselves opportunities to become who we are meant to be. In a relentless effort to be happy and joyous, we dissociate ourselves from anything that looks like sacrifice or service. It is in those moments of discomfort and despair, however, that we grow a tad taller and a bit smarter.

The daily challenges we face are a test of our patience and endurance. Sometimes it's easy to let these temporary distractions rule our world. The spilled milk, the rude driver, the dog eating the homework (it happens—ask any teacher). These tests come part and parcel of the greater trials we encounter along the road.

Loss of a job, loss of identity, loss of a roof over our head, loss of a loved one. The departure for these tests and trials is marked by loss or separation. The initiation phase is the "growth on steroids" part where your world is seemingly destroyed. The return, or reintegration, into the community, comes with a fresh identity, an understated confidence, and a new perspective.

You will endure—and maybe even celebrate—many rites of passage on your Hero's Journey. Some will seem like a rowdy initiation. Others will be of the strong, silent type. The road of trials is where you become more capable and secure. This is where you gain knowledge and wisdom. It is also where you recharge your spirit and live to fight another day.

> "We must be willing to get rid of the life we've planned so as to have the life that is waiting for us. The old skin has to be shed before the new one can come." ~ Joseph Campbell

125

CROSSING THE THRESHOLD

The first trial we face is a big one, the premier rite of passage. Attempting to cross the threshold is where we find out how badly we want to be on this journey, what we're willing to lose in order to gain. The threshold guardian is especially tenacious and diligent at this initial entry point. Successfully crossing the threshold transitions the hero from the ordinary world (conscious mind) to the special world (unconscious mind).

When we come across roadblocks or brick walls in our everyday lives, we find ways to overcome them, or at the very least, we look for a way around them. The limiting forces blocking the hero on this journey are a little more intense. These internal demons and dragons require engagement and confrontation. At various turning points, these guardians show themselves as vices, emotional scars, jealous enemies, and self-limitations.

For Dorothy and her allies in *The Wizard of Oz*, the threshold is the door to the Emerald City. The guardian at Emerald City's gate makes it clear: "Nobody gets in to see the wizard, not nobody, not nohow."

As is often the case in mythology and metaphors, "threshold" has a double meaning. It is not only a passageway, a portal through which we must enter to reach our destination. It is also a measure of endurance, as in our threshold for pain and how long we can persist.

Passing through the threshold of the inner journey involves a subtler internal survival strategy. The hero must outwit, outplay, and outlast the internal foes, rather than do physical battle with them. Not unlike conflicts in the contests of the ordinary world, what gets results may not always be pretty. Craftiness, bribery, deceit, or attacking head-on might be required to take down the hero's shadow. A more discerning approach might be to befriend the threshold guardian, form an alliance, and gather additional tribe members to solve the puzzle or decipher the anagram of life. Until the hero traverses the threshold, life remains a mystery.

Regardless of the strategy chosen, there is no immunity. It is all or nothing.

The threshold guardian is a symbol of the new strength required to enter the special world. Each one encountered provides a blockade, obstacle, or challenge the hero must choose to overcome—and in so doing, they will demonstrate a sincere commitment. The hero's determination, regardless of barriers and deterrents, is tested at a deeper psychological level, subconsciously, by the threshold guardian. This guardian is often not an adversary at all, but a vital character in a pivotal role.

The goal of threshold guardians is to keep us from easily getting what we want and testing our worthiness to ascend to the next level. They will keep us from even getting started on our journey if we let them.

The initial resistance encountered is likely to come from a three-headed guardian named "Doubt, Uncertainty, and Fear." They're not especially mean, but they're a triple threat of the damaging, demoralizing, and devastating kind. Having traveled this path a time or two, I can tell you these guys are a pushover if you know their weakness. Although we spend a considerable amount of time on "I don't think I can," "I'm not sure this will work," and "What if I fail?," the majority of what we worry about never comes to pass. French Renaissance writer Michel de Montaigne noted, "My life has been full of terrible misfortunes most of which never happened."

In the inner world, threshold guardians are best recognized as our demons: depression, anxiety, obsessive behavior. These are the demons that also drive our vices and dependencies, like coffee, chocolate, and doughnuts. Or cigarettes, alcohol, and drugs. The most threatening threshold guardian is our self-limitations.

Threshold guardians are formidable and many. Conquering them requires plans and strategies.

One strategy for successfully navigating the road of trials is to take the offense. Don't let life happen to you; make it happen on your terms. Don't just wait for obstacles to show up and scan for potholes to avoid. Embrace the challenges; get creative.

In another scene from *The Wizard of Oz*, the Tin Man, Cowardly Lion, and Scarecrow attempt to rescue Dorothy from the castle of the Wicked Witch of the West. The legion of marching and chanting soldiers aren't just going to drop the drawbridge and invite them in. Rather than fight a battle they know they cannot win, Dorothy's allies commandeer uniforms and weapons, enabling them to shapeshift into soldiers and march straight into the castle undetected. That's offense with a twist.

How many people do you know who are playing nothing but defense? Their only goal is to make it through the day. Somehow they manage to do so, only to wake up the next morning to suffer through it all again, one more time. And then another. And another.

They're playing defense, and *man* is it tiring. News flash: Life isn't meant to be survived. Playing it safe isn't going win the game. Let's be honest—nobody makes it out of this alive. At some point, the "season" ends. So, if that's the case, why not thrive while you're here? Why not score a life well lived?

Eleanor Roosevelt traveled a very long and arduous road of trials and faced many threshold guardians. Her advice? "Do one thing every day that scares you." In the game of life, the best defense is a good offense.

The most powerful guardians keeping us from passing through the threshold and claiming our destiny are our fears and doubts. The hero's imperfections mirror mankind and the nature of the human condition. In the famous words of cartoonist Walt Kelly, written for his comic-strip character Pogo, "We have met the enemy, and he is us."

GARRISON OF GUARDIANS

The universe sent out a casting call for me to write a book about my experiences on the inner journey. We could all benefit from a map, so I figured, why not? I first answered this call six years ago and eagerly signed on to do the starring role.

I recently sold a successful business I had built over the course of a decade. I didn't have to work a real job. The time was right to indulge myself in the notion of being a writer. Life was good. In fact, it was *easy*.

By now, you know enough about the Hero's Journey to appreciate that easy is not necessarily desirable. I was in a position to do whatever I wanted—or nothing.

What do you think happened? Human nature.

I did nothing for five years. That's not to say my Genie subconscious didn't put a bug in my ear every so often. It wasn't so much a boisterous calling to write this book as it was an incessant tapping on the shoulder.

Every so often, I'd be reminded of how much front work and research I'd put into the book. I had already written the first part, "Date with Destiny." I had commissioned an illustrator to do the interior drawings, hired a digital artist to design the book cover, and paid an editor to make the darn thing readable.

I took notes, did research, jotted down pertinent facts, and bookmarked interesting articles. I outlined the entire journey (or what there was up to that point) and prepared a book proposal. After I had completed the first four chapters, all work stopped.

I was getting kicked in the teeth by various threshold guardians. I'd keep getting up and going forward like you're supposed to, but I also wondered if I just needed to catch a clue and walk away from something that wasn't meant to be.

One threshold guardian came in the form of a tele-class I taught. You'd think with all the experience I had directing a coach training school, the class would have been a slam dunk. It bombed. One participant even wanted their money back.

Another guardian challenging me at the gates of authorship was the process itself: not having good writing days (which were most of them), dealing with an editor who constricted my voice, and negotiating with an intellectual-property attorney who cramped my style. It seemed like the threshold guardians were ganging up on me.

The guardian who gave me my biggest trouncing, however, is a man I still respect and admire. In fact, had there been a hooded robe in the closet, it would have fit him perfectly as far as I was concerned.

I had the good fortune to participate in a writer's retreat held at Jack Canfield's oceanfront home in Maui. Jack and fellow creator of the *Chicken Soup for the Soul* series, Mark Victor Hansen, hosted this small group workshop. I remember handing my book proposal to Jack at one of the breaks and was so looking forward to his glowing comments, enthusiastic encouragement, and unwavering support. Those never came. The rest of the week went by without so much as a word.

This one knocked the wind out of me, and I didn't get up for a long time. I really thought I had something special. It turned out that it was nothing at all. After getting the crap beat out of me by a garrison of guardians, I agreed with them all—writing this book was not meant to be.

At that moment, it became so clear to me. The first hint I received from the universe was almost like a whisper. I paid it no attention. The next suggestion was like a tap on the shoulder: "You don't really want to pass this way. Put the book down." Not really wanting to notice that tap, or the ones after that, I ignored all "recommendations" and continued to persevere. The final directive was no mere hint or suggestion. It felt more like a 2x4 upside the head, followed by, "You will not pass this way."

I put the book down.

The forced sabbatical found me questioning everything. Wasn't I supposed to write this book, or was this a false calling? Was I smart to walk away from something that wasn't working, or was I just refusing the call? It was all so confusing, and in situations like this, we never know for sure. Looking back, the only thing I can figure is that I hadn't lived enough of the journey yet to be judged worthy of writing it and passing through the threshold.

Here we are now, as I write these words, six years later. It feels different now and hard to describe, but somehow it feels *right*. It's not like I was given the green light and all of a sudden started typing away, words a-flowing. I still question why I'm writing the book. Does answering this second call fall in line with who I am now, who I've become? Are the words flowing because it's time, or is it temporary? If the book is successful, do I want to eat, sleep, and breathe this topic for many years to come? What is my fate?

A calling is never simple. A true calling can be downright confusing. There are always questions, even when things are going well—especially when things are going well. Sometimes we just need to play the hand we were dealt and hope like hell we can bluff the threshold guardian into granting us passage.

EXPLORING YOUR ROLE

The road of trials is about testing your resolve while maintaining your integrity. Knowing the right thing to do doesn't always result in doing the right thing. As Morpheus told his protégé in *The Matrix*, "Neo, sooner or later you're going to realize, just as I did, that there's a difference between knowing the path and walking the path."

Be willing to trade modest amounts of joy and happiness for a bounty of courage and heroism. Use your passion, purpose, and plans to outsmart the threshold guardians attempting to deny your destiny.

- Adversity doesn't build character; it reveals it.

- Delaying rites of passage stunts opportunities for growth and life mastery.
- Demons and dragons abound. Confront your demons and train your dragons.

Avoiding the pain of growth means you avoid growing. Suck it up. Step into your true self. When you're not growing, you're dying. Greek historian Herodotus avowed, "Death is a delightful hiding place for weary men."

Getting knocked down reveals you're human. Getting back up reveals your character.

"The world ain't all sunshine and rainbows. It's a very mean and nasty place, and I don't care how tough you are, it will beat you to your knees and keep you there permanently if you let it," growled Rocky Balboa. "You, me, or nobody is gonna hit as hard as life. But it ain't about how hard you hit. It's about how hard you can get hit and keep moving forward . . . how much you can take and keep movin' forward."

Going forward on the road of trials, you become more capable and secure. The road is where you gain knowledge and wisdom. It's where you walk your talk, or wish you had. It's not easy, nor is it intended to be. At times, it will be painful and grueling. Without traversing the road, however, you come no closer to your destination.

✍ Self-Discovery ✍

1. Are you willing to give up the life you've planned so you can have the life that is waiting for you?
2. Can you embrace the tests, tasks, and trials presented to you as rites of passage?
3. Where in your life are you playing defense? What would it look like if you switched to offense?
4. What one thing will you do today that scares you?

CHAPTER 10

THE ORDEAL

*The very cave you are afraid to enter turns out to
be the source of what you are looking for.*
~ Joseph Campbell

The ordeal is about life and death, as well as death and rebirth. Myths and movies mark the gravity of this central conflict with visceral images and compelling prose. However, myths, movies, and magic are not to be taken at face value. They are metaphors and misdirections meant to shock you into thinking differently (not literally). The ordeal you face is a metaphorical life and death, and will kill you or make you stronger (or both).

133

Even children's movies deal with life and death. Disney's *Sleeping Beauty* has a princess on life support until the kiss of a prince changes everything. Charming. From the same studio, Snow White dies from the poison of an apple until the kiss of a prince changes everything (yeah, I know, they're working on new material).

Dorothy suffers her own temporary death before reaching the Wizard of Oz. Author L. Frank Baum constructs his heroine's road of trials out of yellow bricks. One of the many obstacles Dorothy must overcome on her journey to the Emerald City is the field of scarlet-red poppies. "Aren't they beautiful?" she asks her fellow travelers as she breathes in the delicious scent. Little does she know, the Wicked Witch of the West has put a deadly, dark spell on the field of flowers. The author goes on to describe: "their odor and fragrance is so strong and so powerful, that anyone who breathes it in instantly begins to fall asleep, and if the sleeper is not carried away from the deadly scent of the blossoms, they sleep on and on forever and ever until their dying day."

Dorothy collapses into eternal slumber. Ultimately, she is resurrected with the help of her good-witch mentor Glinda, who—with a flick of her magic wand—causes it to snow, dissipating the noxious odors. Death and rebirth.

Destination – *Life and Death*

Let's arrive at an understanding of the metaphorical death and rebirth of the hero. Life-and-death decisions reach their zenith in the ordeal. The Latin root of *cide* (as in decide, suicide, pesticide) means "to kill" or "cut off." When you decide, you have cut off all other options. If this part of the journey is killing you, you're doing it right.

Fellow Travelers – *Shadow, Trickster*

Shadow and Trickster may seem like a couple of guys we don't necessarily want as traveling companions, but we do. Shadow is our dark side and lives deep in the unconscious vault that stores "behaviors that must not be named." Trickster draws attention to imbalance and presents alternatives to stagnant perspectives. These are the companions who identify and gain access to the things we want to change.

The trickster is a mischief-maker, joker, and clown. He keeps things in proportion and shows the hero what not to do by doing it himself. The Genie in Disney's animated film *Aladdin* is an example of a trickster, shapeshifter, and mentor all rolled into one. His razzle-dazzle, flimflam ways often turn out to be an asset to the hero when he is up against opponents who are stronger and more powerful.

The shadow is the worthy opponent representing the energy of the dark side. Shadows appear as villains and bad guys, monsters and aliens, devils and vampires. Ultimately, they dedicate themselves to the defeat, destruction, or death of the hero. It's not difficult to name the shadow character in *Star Wars*. Darth Vader has come to represent the epitome of the archetype. A shadow figure in *The Lord of the Rings* is Gollum, or Sméagol, as he was originally known.

The shadow archetype is most frequently a negative entity representing things we don't like and, at the same time, our darkest desires. You may recognize this character as a familiar shadowy side of yourself that struggles over bad habits and enslaving vices. The shadow symbolizes all that we would like to eliminate. By contrast, the shadow can also be affirmative, representing qualities that have been repressed or not acknowledged. Whether positive or negative, the shadow represents everything we repress and deny within ourselves.

The shadow is hard to conquer because it is every bit as strong as the hero and can match the hero's moves step for step. The shadow sees itself as the hero of its own myth, fighting just as hard for the truth in which it believes. The hero can only be as strong as his most powerful adversary, and the shadow ultimately brings out the best in the hero.

Personal Guide – *Character*

The guide of character is one to be admired. This personal assistant stands tall and most represents the person you want to become. What you desire is already inside you, so look to your character when times get tough and situations get out of hand.

Character is thoroughly tested in the ordeal. The trickster's role is to disrupt; the shadow's role, to destroy. The status quo has no place here, and change is imminent. The mission is to kill and cut off what's not working in our lives. How we respond to the ordeal determines who we become.

There's an old saying: "Be careful what you say, it affects how you think; be careful what you think, it determines what you do; be careful what you do, it determines your character; be careful about your character, it determines your destiny." The life we have lived thus far has generated the person we are and the character we have. Who will you become?

> "Character cannot be developed in ease and quiet. Only through experience of trial and suffering can the soul be strengthened, ambition inspired, and success achieved." ~ Helen Keller

TRIAL BY ORDEAL

Throughout the road of trials, you worked through a series of tests and challenges, each new obstacle more intimidating and formidable than the last. You took a leap of faith and pushed past the threshold guardian. You made mistakes and endured misfortunes. You made new allies and battled old enemies. Your spiritual skin is a bit tougher now, and your inner strength is at an all-time high. This is the time and the place to demonstrate your prowess.

The ordeal is the final and most daunting trial—the reason you have journeyed so far.

The ancient judicial practice of trial by ordeal is a primitive but efficient means of determining guilt or innocence. The accused is subjected to distasteful and dangerous tests that are unpleasant and painful, resulting in life or death. Olympian gods and other celestial entities were believed to control the trial and could intervene on behalf of the accused. Surviving the ordeal was the only proof of innocence.

The central conflict, as it is known in the movie business, marks the midpoint in the film. Luke Skywalker and his allies rescue Princess Leia, but Darth Vader kills Obi-Wan Kenobi.

Agents ambush Neo and his fellow travelers in the Matrix.

Dorothy kills her second witch in a row with the help of a bucket of water.

For us on the inner journey, the ordeal is why we attempted this quest in the first place. The goal is becoming aware of the significant change taking place, facing our shadows and demons, and returning with a renewal of spirit to share in our conscious world. The death of our former identity opens space for a rebirth of the real hero in us.

Done right, life is an ordeal.

Everything that happens on the quest leads to this moment—the ordeal. Everything afterward is about returning home. And, as we all know, there's no place like home.

After overcoming the ordeal, we'll be halfway there. There is more exciting action to come. There are those who would steal our reward, take our elixir, or snatch our broomstick. But we'll leave those adventures for another day. Right now, we must prepare for our greatest challenge as we approach the darkness of the second major threshold.

APPROACHING THE INMOST CAVE

In myths and movies, approaching the inmost cave is what happens on the way to the big battle, the major confrontation, or the location of the main action scene. For Luke and friends, it's when their ship is pulled into the Death Star, where Princess Leia is held prisoner. The life-and-death battle commences shortly thereafter when rescuing the princess.

The crucial destination for the hero in each of us is the inmost place of our being—deep in our unconscious. Some call it the belly of the beast. Others say it is our soul. Bring light into this world and become enlightened by what you discover.

If tempted to ask what's in there, know that it is only what we bring with us. This is our inner journey. We are in control. We are responsible. The things feared are only what we don't understand. Seek to understand, and you are halfway home.

When I finally earned my Bachelor's degree late in life, I began flirting with the idea of going to graduate school. You should have heard my inner demons laughing at that one. The guy who barely made it out of high school and faked his way through college thinks he's attending a top-ranked graduate school where only the best students go? The message from my demons and doubters was loud and clear: *don't push your luck.*

My big battle—my ordeal—would be earning a Master's degree in education; the biggest challenge I had ever attempted. At that point in my professional career, I was giving a talk to the local chapter of Mensa. The entire auditorium was filled with members who scored higher than the 98th percentile in IQ. I told them I wasn't sure they had brought in the right guy to be their speaker. I confessed I graduated in the half of the class that made the top half possible.

The approach to this inmost cave was taking the Graduate Record Exam (GRE). This is the test they give you to see if you're smart enough to even enter the program. As you've probably surmised by now, I don't test well. This was the mother of all tests.

After prepping like crazy and studying for it the best I could, I faced my fears and took the exam. The results letter that came in the mail was bad news and good news. I did not achieve a high enough score to warrant acceptance into the program. However, they would accept me as a provisional student meaning if I had passing grades in the first semester, I could stay.

That's all they had to say. I aced the first semester and never looked back.

The ordeal is best viewed as the second threshold. Just as we prepared to push past the first threshold guardian to enter the special world of the unconscious, we now prepare for the major conflict of this quest: confronting our inner demons and dragons.

We have gradually adjusted to being on the "inside," but being this deep into the unknown is disquieting. We realize what we must do and accept the risks involved—including the one where the dragon we've come to slay manages to live to fight another day. We know this dragon. We'll soon call him by name.

We are approaching the deepest and darkest part of the journey. The commanding leader of the demons is a fire-breathing dragon known as the shadow. The shadow figure feels completely at home on the dark side. Being this close to the controllers of our lives is a bit unnerving, especially since we're on their turf.

The stakes are high. Fears run rampant. To overcome the greatest of all tests, the hero summons skills, training, and experience garnered thus far on the quest. To affect change requires cutting off the pieces that are holding us back from being the best version of ourselves. Prepare to seize the sword.

We know the shadow more intimately than first imagined. There's a reason it's called a shadow, after all. The shadow is our evil twin, the enemy within, the Hyde to our Jekyll. The shadow archetype embodies the thing we don't like about ourselves, that we deny, that we wish no one to know.

As we make our approach to the inmost cave, it's time to regroup the entourage, determine an A-1 strategy, and prepare a

Plan B second strike (if needed). There's no reason to look back. No matter how heroes try to escape their fate, sooner or later the exits are closed off and the life-and-death issue faced.

The Japanese believe that it is only by overcoming an ordeal that we can find meaning that touches our soul. The simple truth to the ordeal is this: Heroes must die so that they may be reborn.

Resurrection calls for a sacrifice by the hero. Something must be surrendered, such as an old habit or belief. Metaphorically, we are coming to terms with our flaws. Something must be sacrificed, given back, or released. The impending ordeal is the turning point. Everything is about to change and—regardless of the outcome—the hero will never be the same.

> "Dark and difficult times lie ahead. Soon we must all face the choice between what is right and what is easy." ~ Professor Dumbledore, *Harry Potter and the Goblet of Fire*

DARK NIGHT OF THE SOUL

In the darkness, we now see things not meant for the light of day. Ironically, we now see more clearly the habits that are holding us back, the beliefs that are not serving us, and the image caused by constant negative self-talk.

In most action-adventures, the ordeal is a dangerous physical test that the hero undergoes while facing a foe. As far as the inner journey is concerned, our greatest ordeal is facing our fears.

The *dark night of the soul* is a term that refers to a disintegration of a perceived meaning of life. It is the transition where we lose the cultural and conditioned meanings we have built up over a lifetime, and it triggers a major reset. The time when our internal system is rebooting (in all probability, much longer than one night) is scary because life no longer has meaning. Depression sets in for no apparent reason. We'd snap out of it if we could, but we just can't put our finger on the source. This is because we are not experiencing a clinical depression caused by external forces. The spiritual depression from which we suffer comes from within.

The pain we feel is real. If your experience is similar to mine, the pain has been real for quite some time. The only way out of this pain—the only way out of the darkness—is going through it. Sounds counterintuitive, doesn't it?

The logical thing to do is back away. The pain, however, only grows larger the more we ignore it or try to suppress it.

For the hero, this is the confrontation with our shadow selves. The biggest casualty is likely to be the death of the ego—no small feat. Regardless of the outcome, life changes forever.

Issues and problems we feel are important and significant no longer seem to matter. Our accomplishments and successes, the quantity and quality of our possessions, the number of friends and contacts we've accumulated on social media. Meaningless. Inconsequential. Trivial.

Everything we hold dear, especially our ego, is endangered. It will kill us to go through with this, and it should. We're cutting off a major piece of our identity that has dominated our existence for decades. Our fear is that we won't be able to live without it. We are correct.

Only through a symbolic death can we experience a metaphorical resurrection that empowers us to fulfill our destiny. Rest assured, my hero—things will lighten up but not before the onset of total darkness.

If we're looking for the culprits responsible for this, we don't have to look far. The shadow and trickster have been working overtime to bring us to this inmost cave. No, it doesn't feel good, but these fellow travelers are doing this *for* our own good. Consider it an intervention. Regard them as adversaries if you want to. We have permission to treat them as hostile if it makes us feel better. Our personal enlightenment and spiritual growth are on the line.

This duo is a double whammy. Shadow shows us who we'd rather not be, and Trickster shows us what not to do by doing it.

"Our shadow controls how much success we're entitled to create or how much failure we're doomed to experience," says author and coach Debbie Ford. "The shadow is an oracle that predicts all of our behaviors, driving the way we treat those around us—and how we treat ourselves."

Shadows are known to be seductive, luring the hero into danger. When the hero needs to perform, it is the shadow that infuses crippling doubts at the critical moment. When crucial steps need to be taken but fear and hesitancy rule the day, those footprints belong to the shadow.

The trickster's role is to disrupt. That's going to look a lot like failure at this point of the journey. The energy of the trickster is that of a contrarian. He is cunning and shrewd while seeming disheveled and irresponsible. Tricksters are adroit at cutting big egos down to size and drawing attention to imbalance and stagnation. They love their role and perform it with a heightened sense of amusement, frivolity, or at the very least, a silly look on their face. The Lakota legends are especially rich in trickster myths like those of Coyote and Iktomi (the latter also being a shapeshifter).

In Hawaiian mythology, the trickster is Māui, an ancient chief said to have created the group of Polynesian islands Americans now call their 50th state. He did this by tricking his brothers while fishing. Māui pretends to have landed a "big one" by catching his hook on the ocean floor. While his brothers try to pull the fish to the surface, they don't notice the islands rising behind them. It's the stuff movies are made of as our friends at Disney so adeptly demonstrate in their 2016 animated film, *Moana*. Māui (voice of Dwayne Johnson) reluctantly joins Moana (Auli'I Cravalho) on her mission to become a wayfinder, like her ancestors who sailed 3,000 years before her.

Tricksters are good at making us laugh at ourselves by altering the status quo, and in the process, necessitating much-needed change.

SHADOW BELIEFS

We define our self-worth and decide our value within society based on a belief system we've built over the years. We may believe we're a great problem-solver, or that we have a great smile and winning personality, or that we're a good team leader or the life of the party. We form an identity that allows us to stand out and be significant. It can even be something as simple as being a good listener or someone who's always punctual. Whatever two or three traits with which we identify most become the fundamental building blocks of our identity.

Our definitions, however, are not synonymous with self-worth and value. The source of the traits we identify with most (e.g., dependable, trustworthy, loving) derives from the antithesis of what we profess to be.

The very opposite of what we identify within ourselves is born from an event in our childhood. For example, "I can't trust anyone. I'm not worthy of love."

The reason experiences in our childhood leave such an indelible mark on our soul is because, at such a young age, we're not able to process events like we do when we're older. As children, we make them mean something about us. Then, since it's all about us, we start drawing conclusions about what that makes us.

The shadow's role is to destroy. It does so by hacking into our belief system. This subtle yet powerful point of manipulation impairs our ability to see ourselves as we really are—both good *and* bad. Lack of consciousness cripples our critical-thinking skills and decision-making capabilities.

"I'm not good enough. If only I were special. Something's wrong with me. I'm such an outsider. I don't deserve to be loved. I'm not worthy." The shadow works in tandem with the ego, building a mountain of doubt about the strength of the building blocks you've been using to construct your character.

While we might feel like we're winning this battle, the unseen impact of this manipulation is the significant shift of focus—from building a life of significance and value to protecting an identity we're not convinced is real. Instead of enlightening and empowering us, our revised beliefs fall into the shadows, weakening our gifts and talents. We go from kicking ass on offense to covering our ass playing defense.

Shadow beliefs are the stronghold of the opposition. They are the fire-breathing dragons we must slay. They command and control our lives from behind the firewall of our unconscious mind. Lacking direct access, we are limited in our ability to consciously change what's not working for us. From the safety of the unconscious mind, the shadow feeds our subconscious mind disinformation and propaganda designed to alter our source code at the core level.

Unconscious beliefs and expectations influence our relationships. How we treat others—and more importantly, how we treat ourselves—determines our quality of life. This, in turn, drives subsequent behaviors. It becomes routine to enter the reality distortion field convincing ourselves we're much better off than we are—or that we're much worse off than is true.

In our defense, we create stories that allow us to rationalize why we're not all we could be. Our justifiable weaknesses and limitations somehow point to why, if things were different, we'd be great. We spend so much time crafting our cover story that we neglect to see how it is keeping us small.

We spend a lifetime under the spell of illusion and delusion— tricking the mind and betraying our beliefs. Delusion is when we know something is false and choose to believe it's true, anyway. Believing we are something we are not is delusional. The easiest person to fool is ourselves, especially when Shadow is performing the illusion. Trickster loves this part and participates as the magician's assistant.

Standing at the threshold of the firewall protecting the unconscious mind is the three-headed guardian of Doubt, Uncertainty, and Fear. Standing directly behind Fear, mostly hidden and cowering, is Ego. Considering its fragility, Ego is remarkable in its overcompensating abilities to prove what is untrue to perpetuate the status quo.

Analogous to the man behind the curtain pulling the levers, toggling the switches, and bellowing into the microphone—it's all smoke and mirrors. The enemy is not the giant wizard head projected amidst the fire and steam, but the fragile ego behind the controls pushing our buttons.

Wounded as a child, Ego has found a safe place from which to control our destiny. Standing on the shoulders of Fear, deep in the labyrinth of the unconscious, Ego keeps us from being who we really are, living in our essence, living from the heart. To do so would be its downfall and death.

The constant flow of negative messages is designed to keep us disoriented, discouraged, and distraught. With all of this in our face, we are more likely to be scrambling for self-preservation than mounting an attack on the status quo. This is precisely where Ego wants us.

The dark night of the soul is the death of the old you and the rebirth of the true you. What does that look like? According to Hollywood script consultant Michael Hauge: living in one's essence. We'll talk more about essence later, but right now we're in the middle of an ordeal.

Even though the death is metaphorical, it is no less painful. What we give up, the identity we lose, the comforts we cut off, hurt like nothing we've ever experienced. It is intangible, but oh so real. This is also a time upon which we will look back and recognize the transformation as necessary to our spiritual awakening.

> "Every man dies. Not every man really lives."
> ~*Braveheart*

PURGING EMOTIONS

The ordeal brings up a full basket of emotions (e.g., love, hate, joy, happiness, anger). These emotions interweave through a complex nervous system triggered by numerous and varied actions and reactions. As we carry this heavy basket along our chosen path, we take solace in the experiences of others: the more dramatic, the better. We know these as stories.

Films, especially, have a way of sneaking up and touching your heart—or pouncing on your soul without warning. *It's a Wonderful Life, Good Will Hunting*, and *The Notebook* exemplify masterful movie-making with maximum tug on the heart strings and an occasional visceral assault on the soul.

Some will inspire you; others may make you mad or frustrated. At times you'll be laughing uncontrollably; at other times you'll be crying your eyes out. Rarely can you leave a well-made film without the emotional experiences staying with you long after you leave the theater.

In *Saving Private Ryan*, three brothers lie dead on the battlefield, with a fourth deep in German-held territory, as Allied forces storm Omaha Beach on D-Day. Captain Miller (Tom Hanks) and his seven men are given orders to go behind enemy lines to locate Private James Ryan (Matt Damon), the sole surviving brother. General George Marshall states in a letter to the mother of the four boys, "Nothing, not even the safe return of a beloved son, can compensate you, or the thousands of other American families, who have suffered great loss in this tragic war."

Saving Private Ryan portrays the moral dilemma of risking the lives of an entire patrol of men to save the life of one low-ranking soldier. It is about the price paid to do the morally heroic thing by finding Private Ryan and safely returning him back home.

> Captain Miller: James Francis Ryan of Iowa?
>
> Private Ryan: Yes, sir. Paton, Iowa, that's correct. What's this about?

Captain Miller: Your brothers were killed in combat.

Private Ryan: Which . . . which ones?

Captain Miller: All of them.

When Private Ryan learns he can go back home he refuses.

Private Ryan: Hell, these guys deserve to go home as much as I do. They've fought just as hard.

Captain Miller: Is that what I'm supposed to tell your mother when she gets another folded American flag?

Private Ryan: You can tell her that when you found me, I was with the only brothers I had left. And that there was no way I was deserting them. I think she'd understand that.

There's something about being swept up and away by a film that is thrilling yet humbling at the same time. What we want from a *good* story is drama, excitement, and emotion. What we get from a *great* story is catharsis.

A Greek word meaning "cleansing" or "purging," *catharsis* is a term used in dramatic art to describe an emotional cleansing depicted in good entertainment or great art. In motion pictures, the phenomenon occurs when one or more of the characters is also part of the audience's experience. We feel what the character feels. Author and literary critic F. L. Lucas takes the definition a step further: "It is the human soul that is purged of its excessive passions."

Catharsis enables the release of pent-up emotions and tensions. Catharsis is any extreme change in emotion that results in relief, renewal, and restoration. Crying is a form of catharsis.

Aristotle was the first to use the term in his work *Poetics*, in response to Plato's claim that poetry encourages people to become hysterical and uncontrolled. Aristotle's position was that literature provided an emotional release linked to a need to uncover unconscious conflicts.

Since the time of the Greeks and Romans, catharsis has taken on many forms and formats. *Braveheart, Field of Dreams*, and *The Shawshank Redemption* all provide a catharsis in different ways. And isn't that why we keep going back to the movies, in hopes of experiencing a transforming, spirit-freeing release of emotion? At the beginning of a *good* story, we hope the main characters will change. At the end of a *great* story, we realize we are the ones who have changed.

"There is no coming to consciousness without pain. People will do anything, no matter how absurd, in order to avoid facing their own soul," noted Carl Jung. "One does not become enlightened by making imaginary figures of light, but by making the darkness conscious."

Like the manipulating of our emotions (which we love so much) in our films, our souls need a cathartic experience just as much, if not more. Hence, the reason for the ordeal.

Maybe this is why we encourage Hollywood to synthesize and administer the emotional drug of catharsis into our movie-going experience. If we could allow our dark souls to cry—even for just a minute—what relief that would bring to our being. The purging of emotions illuminates our new direction down a path of enlightenment.

EXPLORING YOUR ROLE

The ordeal is a rite of passage—the greatest trial you face on your journey—complete with tricksters, egomaniacs, and the deeply embedded beliefs of the shadow. It is here you must stand true to the height of your character.

Shadow beliefs are those which hinder you from being your best. You hold them deep inside, yet they remain outside our conscious awareness. Shining a light on those beliefs softens the shadows. The brighter your light, the less shadow there is, until the shadow belief can no longer exist.

In mythology, the ordeal signifies the death of the ego. The hero places the larger collective above self-interest. Death is the self-surrender and transition from an ego sense of self to connectedness of all things. If this sounds like a movie, it is. The Hero's Journey is the template. Specifically, the hero's inner journey toward a life well lived.

- Done right, life is an ordeal.
- Heroes are only as strong as their mightiest adversary.
- Enemies lure us to the dark side. Our hidden weapon is our inner light.

It can be easy—almost reassuring in a strange way—to commiserate with others on how exhausting life is and why we're not getting ahead. It's a bit tougher, yet far more rewarding, to push forward in the direction of our dreams, even if it's only a step or two.

Those who believe the good life should be easy and carefree are going to be the unhappiest and probably already are. The never-ending challenges and struggles . . . the countless obstacles and conflicts . . . meeting the needs and desires of fortunate loved ones . . . desiring to meet the not-so-fortunate ones who just need love.

A certain amount of friction is necessary in our lives to provide enough heat to mold our minds and cast our mettle to shape the legend we become.

When we finally experience those moments of adrenaline pumping through our veins and the euphoria of life buzzing through our bodies, know that it comes in direct proportion to the challenges we meet, the obstacles we overcome, and the number of people we help along the way.

"Be kind, for everyone you meet is fighting a hard battle." ~ Plato

≫ Self-Discovery ≪

1. What two or three traits do you identify with most that serve as the building blocks of your identity?
2. If you were to rid yourself of a flaw, what would need to be sacrificed, given back, or released?
3. What was happening for you in the last movie you saw where you experienced a catharsis?
4. When your back is against the wall, is it your ego that's pulling your levers and pushing your buttons?

CHAPTER 11

TRANSFORMATION

*Just as a snake sheds its skin, we must
shed our past over and over again.*
~ Buddha

In the *Matrix* trilogy, Morpheus (Laurence Fishburne) tutors Neo (Keanu Reeves) in the ways of what he calls the "real world." Morpheus wants to help shape Neo's destiny by revealing the dream, the Matrix.

In Greek mythology, Morpheus is the messenger of the gods who appears in the dreams of kings. He fashions and molds, shapes and forms the dreams of those who need to change. The modern-day word *morphing* refers to the smooth transformation of one image into another.

In this allegory, the Matrix is the ordinary world that is completely controlled by hidden forces. "It is the world that has been pulled over your eyes to blind you from the truth," states Morpheus, "a prison for the mind."

At the beginning of his journey, Neo is asleep. He soon gains awareness and becomes motivated to take action by seeking the truth. In true mentor form, Morpheus tells his charge, "Unfortunately, no one can be told what the Matrix is. You have to see it for yourself."

As we've seen time and again, a good mentor is just not going to give the answers we seek. At best, we receive a choice: the blue pill, or the red pill, for instance. Take the blue pill: Continue living in the dream and believe whatever you want. Take the red pill: Learn the truth and live in the reality that comes with it.

Our hero opts for change—pushing forward, engaging the shadow, and going where the truth leads. Neo takes a leap of faith and swallows the red pill.

With much training, guidance, and a really cool, long black jacket, Neo begins to understand the Matrix in the darkness of the special world.

During Neo's ordeal, he is shot dead. Trinity, an ally representing sacred feminine energy, watches and is horrified. Neo is dead in the world of illusion.

Neo's rebirth comes in the form of a twist on the Disney princess tales. In an act of love and compassion, Trinity kisses Neo and he reawakens at a new level of consciousness. Enlightened in the ways of the real world, his transformation enables him to see the truth.

Destination – *Resurrection and Renewal*

We are arriving at the new and improved hero, reborn to a higher and better self. Accumulated learning sparks regeneration and a resurgence of our life force. By transcending the former self, the hero transforms from discontentment to self-actualization—from ignorance to enlightenment.

Fellow Traveler – *Shapeshifter*

The shapeshifter's primary objective is to compel the hero to question strongly held beliefs and assumptions. While not attached to a particular outcome, the shapeshifter is adroit at deception and can be a formidable ally in your transformation.

By its very nature, the shapeshifter archetype is hard to understand and difficult to pin down. This character changes roles, moods, appearance, and personality at whim. The shapeshifter is distracting and often confusing, making it difficult for the hero to discern this character's alliances and loyalties. This turbulence compels the hero to question strongly held beliefs and assumptions, which is the shapeshifter's primary objective.

As with the other archetypes, any character can take on attributes of the shapeshifter when the need arises. Mentors frequently appear as shapeshifters. Merlin, King Arthur's mentor, changes shape often to aid the cause. The hero can also become a shapeshifter to deceive an enemy or overcome an obstacle.

Personal Guide – *Accountability*

Your guide for transformation is also your accountability partner. Assuming personal responsibility for decisions made and actions taken seems basic and straightforward. It's about admitting your mistakes, acknowledging your weaknesses, and owning your character.

In our finger-pointing society, it's almost a point of gamesmanship to see who can get out of taking responsibility the quickest. "Fearlessness, honesty, and accountability," states life strategist Robert Ohotto, "are seldom found in our culture of blame, litigation, and hypocrisy."

But why would anyone want to give their power away? Taking responsibility means taking control. Those in control command the power.

Accountability is the glue that bonds commitment to results.

Sometimes we don't follow through on our commitments because we have an unconscious block. It's not our fault—or so we'd like to think. Now that we are getting to know ourselves better and have taken a bumpy excursion through our inner landscape, we recognize that those "blocks" are self-made. Bringing unconscious blocks into the light of consciousness starts with awareness. This gets us halfway there. Once we realize we're blocking, we recognize and identify the culprit. Pushing through the rest of the block requires changing our minds—both conscious and unconscious—to being accountable to our commitments.

One of the reasons coaching and mentoring are so effective is because they give us a built-in accountability partner. We say we're going to do something and must be true to our word. Motivation improves, and commitment strengthens. We stay on track, move forward, and get more done in less time. Accountability is the glue that bonds commitment to results.

> "In the long run, we shape our lives, and we shape ourselves. The process never ends until we die. And the choices we make are ultimately our own responsibility." ~ Eleanor Roosevelt

RESHAPING THE HERO

The hero has been through the stages of awareness and change, and now enters the remaining stage of renewal, the final phase of the inner journey. We have traveled from the conscious mind to the unconscious mind and are on the way back.

The transition from change to renewal is transformational. It can only be initiated and achieved by the hero and—only then—

from within. Realizing this comes through learning the truth, accepting the truth, and living the truth.

In the mythological sense, transformation is about resurrection and the final awakening. In a letter to the Romans, Saint Paul proposed, "Be transformed by the renewing of your mind." (Romans 12:1-2) Through the power inherent in the journey, the conscious and unconscious minds have remodeled our inner landscape.

Reshaping the hero begins with how we see ourselves from the inside out. Once we refresh the view, we can do our own shapeshifting. We already know how.

Whenever we start a new job or enter a new relationship, we get a fresh start on how others view us. We get to try on our renewed self with all the recently acquired ruffles and flourishes (knowledge and wisdom). When we return from a rejuvenating vacation or inspiring weekend retreat, we experience a mini-rebirth of renewed vitality. We feel like a new person.

Pushing the reset button all seems worth it now that we're past the ordeal. An unexpected but beneficial byproduct is that both male and female energies are intertwined and expressed through our revised character. Somehow we feel more balanced and robust. Carl Jung dubbed these energies *animus* and *anima*.

The animus is the male element in the female unconscious, the inner masculine of a woman. The anima is the female counterpart in the male unconscious, the inner feminine of a man. Both qualities are necessary for survival and inner balance. Long repressed by society, the Shapeshifter challenges the hero to develop a stronger balance between the internal male and female energies.

Native American shamans are very familiar with the Shapeshifter archetype. The most powerful Navajo deity, Estsanatlehi, "Woman Who Changes," is a fertility goddess known for transformation and immortality. Referred to as the "self-renewing one," Estsanatlehi alters her appearance and changes shapes.

Her favorite transition is her version of bathing in the Fountain of Youth. Whenever she starts to age, Estsanatlehi walks toward the rising sun until she meets her younger self. She then morphs into the newer, blossoming rendition of the Woman Who Changes. Lather, rinse, repeat.

Unfortunately, such an advanced level of shapeshifting is beyond the scope of this book.

MEDIEVAL CHEMISTRY

Most of us want things to be different, but few of us are willing to change. Unlike the snake, we're *not* ready to shed a familiar and comfortable skin. We know that when we change, we outgrow our former selves and must leave something behind.

Part of us dies or, at the very least, is abandoned in favor of a new and better self. There is a price for renewal, and payment is exacted at the point of transformation. Here is an example from mythology and the movies: "The ancient study of alchemy is concerned with making the Sorcerer's Stone, a legendary substance with astonishing powers. The stone will transform any metal into pure gold. It also produces the Elixir of Life, which will make the drinker immortal."

This quote is from a book Hermione finds in the Hogwarts school library in *Harry Potter and the Sorcerer's Stone*. Alchemy is part science, part philosophy, and the medieval forerunner of chemistry. It includes the seemingly magical transformation of base metals into gold, and the amalgamation of a mythical potion granting immortality.

Isaac Newton, best known for being a physicist and mathematician, was also an alchemist. He specifically worked on a process known as *chrysopopeia*: transmuting base metals into gold. The method was also used symbolically in creating the "philosopher's stone."

The philosopher's stone is the correct terminology. However, both the book and the movie are titled *Harry Potter and the Sorcerer's*

Stone in the United States. Publishers and producers weren't sure Americans would get that the philosopher's stone is magical.

Several hundred years before Newton, a Frenchman and alchemist named Nicholas Flamel was credited with discovering the philosopher's stone. He is said to have learned the secret from a man he met on the road to Santiago de Compostela in northwest Spain. If there was a secret formula, it died with Flamel in the year 1418. So much for immortality.

In 1987, Brazilian novelist Paulo Coelho told the story of a powerful chemist who lives in ancient Egypt. He dresses in all black with a falcon perched nearby for hunting game. The alchemist's most prized possessions are the philosopher's stone and the elixir of life.

The internationally bestselling book *The Alchemist* empowers readers while they accompany the Andalusian shepherd boy Santiago, our hero, on his fateful journey to discover his destiny. The book sold more than 65 million copies and holds the world record for the most translated book by a living author (80 languages). It has all the wonderful attributes of a captivating myth: symbolism, allegory, spirituality, and metaphor.

In *The Alchemist*, Santiago receives his call to adventure in a recurring dream he believes holds the key to his destiny. He seeks the guidance of a gypsy fortune-teller before setting off on his quest to discover the treasure of his personal legend.

Dreams are stories you vividly tell yourself while you sleep. They are an integral component of transformation and are worth paying attention to, according to Pulitzer Prize–winning playwright Marsha Norman: "Dreams are illustrations . . . from the book your soul is writing about you."

MISFORTUNE TO FORTUNE

Stories are ingrained in our being whether we're awake or asleep, conscious or unconscious. Most stories, regardless of the medium in which they're told, include a transformation from misfortune to fortune.

What might that look like in the real world?

While writing this book, I've experienced numerous tests and trials, along with a seriously dark night of the soul—one of the benefits of "teaching what you need to learn most." It is challenging to research this topic, examine the issues, and process the findings without taking a hard look at oneself. And, yes, I did say "benefit." Let me explain.

I've always considered myself an outsider. I have never felt like I fit in with the rest of the group. It doesn't matter if it's a neighborhood party, a family reunion, or a group I'm leading. It's strange, I admit.

My family moved around a lot when I was a kid. My father was a chef. Not that being in the food business meant we had to move every few years. Let's just say that, for my dad, the grass was always greener somewhere else. And when I say somewhere else, I'm not talking about moving across town or over to the next city. I'm talking about leap-frogging entire states.

When people ask me where I'm from, it's a hard question to answer. Growing up (and without admitting we had Gypsy blood) it was easiest just to say "the East Coast." From when I was born until the time I graduated high school, I had lived in Maine, Rhode Island, New Hampshire, Pennsylvania (twice), New Jersey (twice), Maryland, and Virginia. At that point, I disembarked from the caravan. My parents and brother continued moving south, eventually stopping in Florida (and only then because they ran out of land mass).

By the time I was 12 years old, I had attended three different elementary schools and four middle schools. I *was* the outsider. Can we talk about being picked last for teams in gym class? It got to the point that I'd enter a new school and not even bother to make friends because I was certain I wouldn't be there that long.

Yes, it was painful as a kid to deal with the teasing and rejection warranted for Norman New Guy. Did it leave a mark?

Sure it did. But here's what happens with shadow beliefs: They shape and mold us, but it doesn't have to be in only a bad way. They also transform us.

Today, I use the outsider identity as an edge, and I have for as long as I can remember. Since I see things differently, it gives me a unique perspective. Offering a different point of view can be an asset. Writing a book, for example, provides me with an opportunity to present a viewpoint that's off the beaten path. Even if you disagree with me, if you're thinking differently from when you began this book, I'm elated.

Consider how your shadow beliefs have enabled you to set yourself apart. Would you be the person you are today without the misfortunes you have endured? As the hero of your journey, you instinctively take the bull by the horns and transform misfortune into fortune.

Most of us will do anything to avoid misfortune. It hardly seems like any good could come from it, but not so. Misfortune is somewhat of a misnomer. Fortune is best derived from misfortune by simply eliminating the "mis"es (*mis*takes, *mis*informed, *mis*guided, *mis*understood). We accomplish this by actually experiencing those misfortunes—one by one—and using the knowledge gained as the building blocks of wisdom. Over time, we become informed, guided, and understood. This is our good fortune.

Rather than repressing and denying shadow beliefs, be grateful for a spin on the wheel of fortune enabling the experience of transformation.

Rota fortunae, meaning "wheel of fortune," is an ancient philosophy referring to the unpredictable nature of fate. The goddess Fortuna spins her wheel at random, changing the positions of those on the wheel. Some are fortunate; others suffer great misfortune.

The Fates are among the eldest goddesses in ancient Greek mythology. The three Fates—Clotho, Lachesis, and Atropos—are daughters of Zeus and Themis, the goddess of justice.

Between the three of them, the Fates determine when you come into this world, how long you'll be here, and when you die. Clotho ("the spinner") spins the thread determining a person's time of birth. Lachesis ("the apportioner") measures the thread defining the length of the person's life. Atropos ("the inevitable"), the cruelest of the three sisters, snips the thread for the exact time of death.

Turning misfortune into fortune is our responsibility. We start by being accountable and then move toward transforming fate.

TRANSFORMING FATE

How much of what we do is predetermined by the "stars" and how much is free will? Or is it all a bunch of malarkey?

The words *fate* and *destiny* are often used interchangeably to represent "what is meant to be." It can be confusing, but the two words mean different things. Here's a quick distinction: Fate is inevitable. What you do with it determines your destiny.

Robert Ohotto, the author of *Transforming Fate Into Destiny*, believes we are both fated and free—that our future is both prewritten and changeable. He says, "Our Fate will bring to us everything we need to fulfill our purpose here; but what we do with what Fate gives us, through our creative power of choice, determines our Destiny."

There are two distinct schools of thought on this topic: those who believe our fate is written in stone and those who believe we choose our destiny. What do the scholars believe? Many dictionaries list fate as a synonym for destiny (along with karma and kismet), or even use it in their definition of destiny. Here's an example from the Free Dictionary: "des·ti·ny (dĕs'tə-nē) — the inevitable or necessary fate to which a particular person or thing is destined; one's lot."

I don't know about you, but I don't find this helpful or hopeful. Whenever the word being defined is used in the definition, it seems like the publishers don't really know what to tell us and are just spinning a description. For individuals acquiring their first look at destiny, this dictionary definition from 30,000 feet may be helpful. For our purposes, however, a closer look is necessary, and distinctions are indispensable.

Wikipedia offers a more expansive gaze: Destiny may be seen either as a sequence of events that are inevitable and unchangeable, or as something chosen by individuals as they select different paths throughout their life. Of course, there are those who say choosing a different course of action and taking paths will still lead you to a predetermined destiny.

Another way to look at it: You face fate; you define a destiny. We all have a date with destiny, Michael Meade suggests, but must suffer the disappointments of fate in order to arrive. Don't worry, though; it is not as doom and gloom as it sounds.

Fate is what life brings to you.
Destiny is what you bring to life.

Fate can be compared to an electrified fence. When you're drifting off the path of your destiny, count on fate to give you a jolt that sparks your attention and nudges you back on track. You'll find it irritating, but that's where you gather the pearls of wisdom.

Pearls form when an irritant—usually a parasite and not the proverbial grain of sand—works its way into an oyster, mussel, or clam. As a defense mechanism, a fluid is used to coat the irritant. Layer upon layer of this coating, known as nacre, is deposited until a lustrous pearl is formed.

So, which is it? Choice or no choice?

Many Greek legends teach that trying to outmaneuver an inexorable fate is futile. If that's true, there's no control over fate, but is that also the case with destiny? Presidential hopeful and former Secretary of State William Jennings Bryan believed, "Destiny is no matter of chance. It is a matter of choice. It is not a thing to be waited for, it is a thing to be achieved."

While fate and destiny are a pairing, much like peanut butter and jelly, they are distinctly different. Just like a good PB&J sandwich, however, you're more likely to hear about them together, because together they create a dynamic tension that gives our lives meaning and purpose. Ohotto uses the analogy of fate being the cards you are dealt, and destiny, how you play them.

ONE HERO'S DESTINY

The hero's role is to serve and to sacrifice. Consider the role of Michael Corleone, the character played by Al Pacino in *The Godfather*. At the beginning of the movie he is a military hero attending Dartmouth, trying to escape the legacy of the crime family into which he was born. This is the ordinary world for Michael. He assures his fiancé with the words, "That's my family, Kay, that's not me."

The special world centers on Michael's father, Don Vito Corleone, the Godfather (Marlon Brando), who heads one of the five crime families controlling New York in the mid to late 1940s. Don Corleone is a powerful and respected crime boss but is losing power because he disapproves of getting into the business of narcotics.

Michael has always rebelled against the family business and wants no part of it. His call to adventure comes with the assassination attempt on his father. Michael can no longer refuse the call and goes to the hospital to reaffirm loyalty to his father and mentor. Michael crosses the threshold when he discovers the hospital abandoned and his father defenseless against another imminent mob hit. He tells his father, "I'm with you now." He is now firmly ensconced in the special world of the family business. He protects his father and learns Police Captain McCluskey is working for one of the other crime families.

On the road of trials, Michael confronts the corrupt McCluskey and drug kingpin Virgil Sollozzo, the men responsible for the attempt on his father's life. His brother Sonny (James Caan) and adopted brother, consigliere Tom Hagen (Robert Duvall), are Michael's allies in planning the murder of these two enemies. Sonny is concerned Michael is doing this for revenge. Michael assures him, "It's not personal—it's strictly business."

The approach to the inmost cave is the careful planting of the weapon in the bathroom of the Italian restaurant where the ordeal takes place. After much nervousness and tension, Michael shoots both Sollozzo and McCluskey, and drops the gun on the floor as he walks out of the restaurant. More tests, trials, and ordeals follow. When Don Corleone dies of a heart attack, Michael becomes head of the family business, a reward he would never have anticipated, nor wanted, years earlier. The road back to the ordinary world has Michael settling all family business and, symbolically, ascending to his father's throne.

In an ironic twist, the resurrection takes place in church at the baptism of Michael's nephew. While being ordained as godfather to his nephew, his allies assassinate the leaders of the other ruling families and execute all remaining enemies. Cementing a reputation of being more cunning and ruthless than his father, Michael returns with the reward of rebirthing the Corleone family as the most powerful crime family in the country. Michael's journey of transformation (albeit to the dark side) is complete. The new Don Corleone continues the legacy as the Godfather.

The role of the hero is to serve and to sacrifice. On the road of trials, Michael sacrifices who he is and everything he wants to be in order to serve his family. These are sacrifices that last a lifetime and determine his destiny. We may not agree with his choices or approve of his methods, but he is, nonetheless, a hero to the Corleone family. Choosing this path was not Michael's intention, but it was his fate. Ultimately, the choice made in a split second became his destiny.

MOMENTS THAT MATTER

For Michael Corleone, the fateful moment by his father's hospital bedside was the moment he said, "I'm with you now." A seemingly simple act of love totally altered the course of Michael's destiny.

Life changes in an instant. Neurons spark a decision measured in milliseconds, redirecting life in ways we can't possibly predict. One day we can be a promising young college student, but in an instant, we can turn down a precarious road toward a life of crime.

We have but a moment to determine who we really are and what really matters.

Italian poet and novelist Cesare Pavese wrote, "We do not remember days, we remember moments." In truth, moments are all that matter. In reality, moments are all we get.

A moment of joy here, a moment of peace there. A moment of ecstasy, a moment of truth. They come and they go rather quickly, but those are the moments we remember. That's what matters.

The first time you kissed your partner, music that gives you goose bumps, unexpected recognition from someone you admire, your baby's first steps. And let's not leave out the "Big O." All of them, moments that matter.

If you only had 525,600 minutes to live, how would you spend them? Even though that's a high number, it doesn't seem like much time, does it? If I asked the more common question, "What would you do if you only had a year to live?" you might provide me a different response. Both answers, though, are likely to involve more of the moments that matter.

We live for moments. We willingly trade misery for moments. Most of these moments last for less than a minute, yet we will do anything to experience them. It's because those few moments make everything that went into manifesting them all worthwhile. This is what really matters.

Even if the other half million–plus minutes aren't all that great.

EXPLORING YOUR ROLE

All myths are stories of transformation. All stories are about change. The most exciting and inspiring characters in these stories are the ones who change the most. Like us, they don't start out as heroes, but through hard work, sacrifice, and perseverance, they transform the hero within.

Fate may have brought you to where you are now. How well you play the cards fate has dealt you determines your dealings with destiny. The hero within reminds you, "If it's meant to be, it's up to me." And the rest of the maxim should be, "If it's up to me, it's on me."

- Fate is what life brings to you. Destiny is what you bring to life.
- The perils of fate spawn the pearls of wisdom.
- Be true to your word—your soul is listening.
- Accountability is the glue that bonds commitment to results.
- Dreams are stories you vividly tell yourself while you sleep.

Looking back on your journey, you became aware of how we needed to change and did something about it. It was tougher than first imagined (it usually is), but you pushed through your darkest days (or months, or years) and shed an old skin. Entering the final phase of the journey, you are renewing your minds, revealing your gifts, and rejuvenating your spirit.

Spiritual quests have been around since the beginning of recorded history. In modern times, we have honed in on the search for identity. Both are exciting and adventurous expeditions that help us discover who we are and why we're here. Both are a quest for knowledge.

Dr. Wayne Dyer said it most succinctly: "Change your thoughts—change your life." The devil being in the details, of course. In manifesting something new, we must make space for it by getting rid of something that's not working.

Part of us dies, or at the very least, is abandoned in favor of a new and better self. The price for renewal is the loss of a familiar and strangely comfortable yet outdated identity. We are reshaping ourselves from the inside out, and it's starting to look pretty good.

Life is a collection of moments. The special moments in our lives make everything that went into manifesting them worthwhile. Live for the moment.

✑ Self-Discovery ✑

1. Do you have an accountability partner—someone who keeps you motived and committed to results?
2. In the past, how have you transformed tragedy into triumph, misfortune into fortune?
3. If dealing with fate is going to be a regular thing (and it is), how does acknowledging this change things?
4. Which "moments" in your life have been the most meaningful and memorable?

CHAPTER 12

ENDOWMENT

The greatest talents often lie buried out of sight.
~ Plautus, Roman playwright

W ill Hunting is a janitor and construction worker from a blue-collar neighborhood in South Boston. His favorite pastimes are baseball, bars, and his buddies. Will has a gift for math and chemistry but suppresses his potential in favor of fitting in with his working-class friends. He wants Skylar, a Harvard med student who's taken a liking to him, to finish her organic-chemistry homework so they can hang out at the batting cages. Skylar doesn't understand how Will's mind works. Even the smartest people she knows have to study—a lot. To Will, it comes so easily. He attempts an explanation.

167

Will: Did you play the piano?

Skylar: I want to talk about this.

Will: No, I'm trying to explain it to you. You play the piano?

Skylar: Yeah, a bit.

Will: So when you look at a piano you see Mozart.

Skylar: I see "Chop Sticks."

Will: Alright, well, Beethoven. He looked at a piano and it just made sense to him. He could just play.

Skylar: So, what are you saying. You play the piano?

Will: No, not a lick. I mean, I look at a piano and see a bunch of keys, three pedals and a box of wood. But Beethoven, Mozart, they saw it and they could just play. I couldn't paint you a picture, I probably can't hit the ball out of Fenway, and I can't play the piano.

Skylar: But you can do my O-chem paper in under an hour.

Will: Right, well, when it came to stuff like that, I could always just play.

What do you "just play?" Sometimes we forget or neglect our talents, and they drift off into the ether. Other times, in an effort to please, we try making a talent out of something somebody else wishes they had. You spend more time with yourself than anyone else, by a long shot. You know what's best. Trust yourself and nurture your best nature. Now is the time to really tune in to what you "just play" and share it with the world.

Destination – *Knowledge and Wisdom*

It may not be accurate to declare knowledge and wisdom to be your destination. You've been accumulating an understanding of who you are and where you're going for some time now. The application of this knowledge and wisdom comes in the form of boon and bounty.

Fellow Traveler – *Mentor*

Mentor is back with you for this segment of the journey but in more of a train-the-trainer capacity. You are about to take on the mentoring responsibilities inherent in life mastery. Consider it a passing of the baton, as it is now your turn to mentor.

Personal Guide – *Generosity*

The guide of generosity empowers you while you empower others through your kindness, caring, and sharing. The spirit of generosity manifests abundance and goodness in exchange for your gifts and talents—a fair trade your guide joyfully administers.

Generosity is a spiritual value, as well as a spiritual practice throughout the world. It is taught as a core value by all major religions, including Christianity, Judaism, and Hinduism. Generosity is one of the five pillars of Islam. Generosity is also a central pillar of Buddhism. *Dana* (pronounced "dah-na") is the Pali word for generosity and is considered one of the Seven Treasures of Noble Ones. Dating back to the time of the Buddha, it affirms that in the act of giving, we develop an ability to let go, cultivate a spirit of caring, and acknowledge the interconnectedness we all share.

While being generous is noble, there is also genius in it. It's no accident that both words share the same root of *gen*, meaning birth, as in "to generate." Generosity involves generating prosperity and abundance through attitude and actions. It is a transformational cycle of positive energy enlarging the lives of others while magnifying the life of the hero in the process.

> "The meaning of life is to find your gift. The purpose of life is to give it away."~ Pablo Picasso

GIFTS, TALENTS, AND STRENGTHS

You were born to flourish. As you enthusiastically set off collecting meaningful moments, don't miss this one. Your heightened sense of awareness and engagement is illuminating a new you that's open to life as it comes—life as it is meant to be. New insights into your destiny find you willfully embracing the unknown. Or, as *The Motivation Manifesto* author Brendon Burchard puts it, "joyfully unwrapping the gifts that fate has chosen to bring."

Endowments are many and varied. These are just a few: creativity, intuition, empathy, social skills, problem-solving, self-discipline, and artistic endeavors.

Your gifts, virtues, and life skills are temporarily in your care. As they say, you can't take it with you. You may generously pass them on to others, especially those having just received the call. You will soon be the mentor helping shape others with what you have learned.

Knowledge and wisdom are another one of those word pairings that can be confusing. The easiest way to grasp a distinction is to dissect the elements of learning.

1. **Data**: ways of expressing things, facts
2. **Information**: arrangement of data into meaningful patterns
3. **Experience**: application and productive use of information

4. **Knowledge**: practical understanding through experience
5. **Wisdom**: the discerning use of knowledge

The process of data becoming information and information becoming knowledge is at the heart of thinking, communicating, and learning. Wisdom speaks from the soul.

Accumulated wisdom is the discerning use of knowledge over time. This is often accomplished through feelings, instincts, and intuition—the tools of wisdom.

While we're at it, we should make one more distinction—the difference between gifts and talents. "Your talent allows you to have a wonderful career," says comedian Steve Harvey, "Your talent is what you're paid for. Your gift is what you're made for." Purpose and passion emanate from your gift. The deeper reason for your being goes way beyond your talents, but it will take everything you have to achieve your destiny.

Our gifts and talents are inside us just waiting to sing. They get a shout-out every once in a while, but not nearly enough time to belt out the whole song. Ridding ourselves of the doubts and limitations that incapacitate us enables us to embrace the endowments with which we have been entrusted.

GATHERING YOUR GIFTS

If you've been looking for a gift and can't seem to locate it, or if you think you know what it is but you're not quite sure, try looking here: Your gift is in your pain.

When I was young, education was my nemesis. School was the bane of my existence. I was terrible at memorization and didn't test well. For book reports, I would find a book in the library with dust-cover flaps summarizing the story. To expand upon that, I would flip through the book, find a paragraph here, add a caption there, and call it a book report.

In high school, I received special permission to enter a work-study program where I attended only three classes and then went to work at a full-time job. I loved it. I was *doing*, and it felt great. Much better than *being* a student—a poor one, at that.

The educational philosophy I embraced at the time came from Mark Twain, who said, "Some people get an education without going to college; the rest get it after they get out."

It's little more than ironic that a guy who barely makes it out of high school finds his passion in education. The motivation? A growing awareness of learning styles. My style is primarily kinesthetic—I learn by doing. I found myself seeking out experiential learning opportunities and couldn't get enough. I was gifted with a love of learning and pursued it with a passion. There was no way I was going to let schooling interfere with my education. Thank you, Mr. Twain.

It was 20 years before I set foot in my first college classroom. Once I graduated (at the age of 43), it was a breakthrough—not because I had earned a master's degree at a major university but because it wasn't that big of a deal. I had already encountered most of the curriculum in the School of Hard Knocks. I knew from experience what the professors were teaching in theory.

Right then, I dedicated myself to learning and teaching. The experience was transformative. At the time, I didn't realize educating was my gift; I just knew that no one needs to wander around for decades thinking they aren't very smart.

The pain I felt in not being smart revealed my gift. The pain you feel may be just the 2x4 smacking you upside your head letting you know your gift is RIGHT HERE. Don't wait for the better part of your life to pass by before you dig at the source of your pain. The gift you uncover might just surprise you.

RETURNING WITH THE ELIXIR

The noblest goal in all of Western alchemy is discovering the "elixir of life." If a person were to drink the elixir from a specific cup, at a particular time, at regular intervals, they would be granted eternal youth, and quite possibly, immortality. This is the final reward on the Hero's Journey—the boon, the benefit, the bounty.

The hero has endured much pain, faced countless injustices, braved certain danger, and bested impossible odds. To the victor go the spoils.

The final reward on the Hero's Journey is a personalized elixir for which you provide the ingredients and customized chemistry. The prize may come in the form of a magic potion but could just as easily be a great treasure, skills acquired, or newfound wisdom.

These endowments enable you to return to your conscious world and share valuable insights, perspective, and awareness. This is why you are here. This is why you were born. No one else brings your gifts to this world.

Returning with the elixir means you can now heal the wounds of the community, the collective, just as you have healed your own. The life lessons, the hands-on experience, the practical knowledge, all position you to do the most good for the most people in the most amazing way.

GRACE, GOODNESS, AND GRATITUDE

In creating the magic elixir, our inner alchemist mixes healthy portions of awareness, change, and renewal with equal quantities of grace, goodness, and gratitude. In a proprietary methodology, this artful amalgamation also receives a squirt of oxytocin and— *voila*—our own customized elixir of life.

Oxytocin is the chemical in our brain responsible for empathy, or simply put, our ability to appreciate what it must be like to be in the same situation as someone else. When we identify with someone in need, our brains generate a flow of oxytocin. This chemical creation is much like when our brains synthesize endorphins or push adrenaline through our systems to avert danger. With heightened levels of oxytocin, we are more trustworthy, generous, charitable, and compassionate.

So, if the endowment period is all about the giving of your gifts and talents, what's in it for you? That's the "grace, goodness, and gratitude" part.

Oh gee, thanks, right? Don't these sound more like consolation prizes? Think about what you get, though.

Grace is found in the beauty of form, the fluidity of motion, and the elegance of aesthetics. Poise, finesse, and etiquette are graceful endowments, as are dignity, decency, and decorum. We can be graced by someone's presence, and we express joy when exhibiting our own gracefulness.

Goodness is marked by the qualities of moral excellence and virtuous conduct. It is also an inherent trait in many of your personal guides on this journey: truth, integrity, character, and generosity. Goodness is the endowment that promotes living well by doing well.

Gratitude activates the essence of life. Being thankful, showing appreciation, and returning kindness super-charges everything and everyone in its path. Being grateful promotes love and compassion while improving self-esteem, mental vitality, and psychological health.

These sound like the ultimate wish list for a life well lived. Grace, goodness, and gratitude are like the additives you put in the gas tank to make your car perform better, or the vitamins and supplements you take at breakfast to boost your body. Immersing yourself in the elixir of life is as close as one gets to eternal youth and immortality.

EXPLORING YOUR ROLE

Joyfully unwrap the gifts fate has brought you (don't mind the paper cuts). You are the temporary guardian of the talents and strengths you have been afforded. Your endowments enable you to "save the world" to which you return.

Don't forget what you have learned here. Assist in the labor of the mind and birth knowledge and wisdom into your world.

- Purpose and passion emanate from your gifts.
- Nobody else brings your gifts to the world but you.
- Accumulated wisdom is the discerning use of knowledge over time.
- Grace, goodness, and gratitude are the heartbeat of a life well lived.
- Live well by doing well.

At this point, it hardly seems enough to heed the words of our personal guide: "Give more than you take." We benefit so much from the generosity we demonstrate, it almost seems selfish.

Going forward, know that it is impossible to give more than you receive. This becomes all the more evident when you embrace the role of the mentor. We'll delve into this topic next.

⋙ Self-Discovery ⋘

1. What do you "just play?" Start a list of your gifts, talents, and strengths.
2. Which of these endowments are you able to generously pass on to others?
3. Of all your gifts, virtues, and life skills, which is your best? What makes you stand tall and stand out?
4. Considering everything that has happened in your life, for what are you most grateful?

Return with the Elixir
Unlock your gifts and talents.
willcraig.com/gifts

CHAPTER 13

LIFE MASTERY

Do not go where the path may lead you,
go where there is no path and leave a trail.
~ Ralph Waldo Emerson

One of the greatest action-adventure stories ever filmed is *Raiders of the Lost Ark*. The U.S. government hires Dr. Indiana Jones, an eminent archaeologist and antiquities expert, to find the Ark of the Covenant. The Ark is believed to hold the Ten Commandments. Dr. Jones' transformation from a half-dorky college professor to whip-cracking, fedora-wearing action hero is an arc of the cinematic kind. The dual story lines make for great entertainment.

Set in 1936, Indy and his ex-flame, Marion, set off on a quest that takes them from Nepal to Cairo. The fast-paced, comic-book, cliff-hanger, non-stop action-adventure film set a new standard for the genre and became an instant Hollywood classic.

Raiders of the Lost Ark is one of those rare creative endeavors that produces layers of legends. It was the 1981 summer box-office smash and the year's top-grossing film. Harrison Ford, who had already locked in fame with the *Star Wars* films, went on to do three more *Indiana Jones* movies, with a fifth on the way.

Raiders was the first collaboration between the two legendary filmmakers George Lucas and Steven Spielberg. They both happened to be in Hawaii as *Star Wars* was making history of its own. Lucas shared his concept for a movie about a globe-trotting archaeologist and academic named Indiana Smith. Indiana was the name of Lucas' dog, who loved riding in the passenger seat of his car. The Alaskan Malamute was also the inspiration for Chewbacca in *Star Wars*. Spielberg liked the idea but didn't think Smith was the right name for the character. Lucas said, "Okay, what about Jones?"

All three—Ford, Lucas, and Spielberg—are legends in the entertainment industry. They created a legendary character in a legendary motion picture that was nominated for nine Academy Awards and remains one of the highest-grossing films of all time.

Raiders was a win for everyone, especially audience members who joined Indy on his adventures. We were all the hero in that story, even if it was only for 155 minutes. The *Indiana Jones* film series leaves a lasting legacy for everyone involved: the creators, the studio, the cast, and crew. In essence, the storytellers—the mythmakers.

Think about the possibilities for your storytelling. We are all the bona-fide heroes of our own action-adventure—minus the fedora and bullwhip. What do you want your legacy to be?

Destination – *Legend and Legacy*

Arriving at the final destination is an end and a new beginning. Identifying your legend and establishing your legacy are the rewards and renewal you earn. Heralds in the distance trumpet a new call to adventure for the hero with new awareness.

Fellow Travelers – *Heroes, Allies*

If there was any doubt before, as to who is the hero of this story, there is none now. A new you has evolved from the experience of a lifetime. Your friends, colleagues, and other hometown heroes welcome you back to where you began—familiar yet different as seen through fresh eyes.

The hero's inner journey is symbolic of the soul in transformation and represents our individual search for identity and wholeness. As the hero on this quest, we face our demons, dragons, and monsters. We enlist the support of our internal helpers, guides, and mentors. We look inside ourselves and find corruption and cruelty. We also find friends and allies who live within the boundaries of our heart and soul. Our task on this expedition is to assimilate all the seemingly disparate entities within ourselves into a single, congruent, and balanced being. No small task.

Personal Guide – *Guardian Spirit*

The personal guide and guardian for life mastery is your guardian spirit. Heroes still face dangers and evil both from within and without. Your guardian spirit not only protects you, but also inspires the decisions leading to a life well lived.

You are stepping into a new role. The pupil becomes the teacher; the protégé becomes the mentor; the apprentice becomes the master. Returning with the elixir empowers you with knowledge and wisdom—the experiences had, the lessons learned, and the wounds healed.

Having lived and survived in both spheres, you are officially the Master of Two Worlds. You know the geography of the ordinary and special worlds, as well as the currents of the conscious and unconscious minds. You know thyself.

Knowing yourself well, being passionate about your purpose, and living in your essence weaves an exquisite tapestry known as a high quality of life.

> "What you leave behind is not what is engraved in stone monuments, but what is woven into the lives of others." ~ Pericles, Greek statesman and orator

OWNING THE LIFE YOU DESERVE

You've likely figured out that the life you've lived, up till now, is the life you've earned—for better or worse. You are accountable. It's on you. No one else has lived your life—not even for a moment.

The truth is, you already own the life you deserve. If you think you deserve more, then you need to *be* more.

The sum total of everything you bring to the world, the way you play the cards you were dealt, the way you benefit our interconnected humanity—this is your life. You are endowed with the power to improve it. Suffering is optional.

The conquering hero can choose to own a big castle filled with expensive possessions—the more, the merrier. Or, the victor can place the spotlight on owning something far more valuable— a life well lived.

Ownership requires responsibility. And, as we've learned, taking responsibility equals power. Endowed with the gifts and talents we now know we possess, we are in the unique position of living the life we desire. Be careful what you wish for.

You've made the hard choices, completed the challenging tasks, faced your demons, and named your dragons. You know how this works and command the resources to make most anything happen. What do you wish for?

"There are thousands and thousands of people out there leading lives of quiet, screaming desperation," says work/life balance author, Nigel Marsh, "where they work long, hard hours at jobs they hate to enable them to buy things they don't need to impress people they don't like."

Ask any millionaire—or billionaire, for that matter—how important money is in their life and they won't quibble. Like the rest of us, they recognize they wouldn't want to be without it. The wealthy, however, go on to acknowledge that money doesn't deliver all the "riches" they first perceived it would when they were young and foolish.

As you must own the life you deserve, so too, you must own your excellence. Let's face it—you are amazing! There is no one else in the world like you. It's almost too hard to believe, but it's true. You are one of a kind.

You have a gift that you were brought into this world to convey. No one else can deliver it but you. There's just one catch. To fully deliver this gift, to fully live up to your potential, you must own your excellence. You must acknowledge your greatness and all the reasons you are special.

Why is owning our excellence so challenging for most of us? Is it just a matter of confidence?

If self-confidence were all it took, we would, in fact, own our excellence. There's a natural tendency to believe we're not as good as the next guy. We've had to overcome certain obstacles, trials, and tribulations. We must not be as inherently wonderful as the truly dynamic people around us.

Intellectually, we know this isn't true. But somehow, the message doesn't seem to resonate in our core.

Of course, there are certain individuals (and I'm sure you've met a few) who are tremendously self-confident—maybe over-confident—and own more excellence than they deserve. For some reason, they have an over-inflated opinion of their skills and abilities, and are fearless. How do they do that?

We can all take a lesson from these mere mortals. Grab some of that confidence for yourself. Other human beings are people much like you and me. In fact, people are more alike than they are different. There's a better-than-average chance they are not as glorious as they imagine or pretend to be. There is an equally good chance (100%, in my book) that you are much better than you perceive yourself to be. Acknowledge your greatness. Own the life you deserve. Forrest did.

Despite his low IQ and physical restrictions, Forrest excels at living a charmed life. He runs from one encounter to the next, shrugging off limitations and discrimination. Actor Tom Hanks gives an Oscar-winning performance in the title role of the 1994 film *Forrest Gump*.

Life doesn't turn out to be ideal for Forrest (when does it ever?), but it doesn't keep him from being kind, honest, and forthright with everyone he meets. Maybe the most incredible attributes Forrest possesses are courage and confidence. Was Forrest compensating for his weaknesses by demonstrating these virtues, or was he courageous and confident because he didn't know any better? It doesn't matter, does it? Either way, he owned the life he deserved.

"Run, Forrest, run!"

YOUR PERSONAL LEGEND

Striving to develop a personal legend sounds a little egocentric. It appears to run counter to our purpose, especially since we just spent an enormous amount of time and energy trying to transcend the ego and integrate it into our being.

Yes, it's true that a personal legend could be used for less-than-altruistic reasons. But in living the Hero's Journey, our purpose is self-actualization: living in essence.

Self-actualization is a human need, as are esteem, love, shelter, food, and water. Gaining fulfillment through achieving our potential ranks at the top of the hierarchy. The trouble is, if we're homeless, don't have enough to eat, and our safety is constant jeopardy, self-actualization isn't anywhere close to top-of-mind awareness.

A formalized framework of human needs comes from Abraham Maslow. In *Motivation and Personality*, published in 1954, he describes the stages of personal growth and the path that human motivations follow.

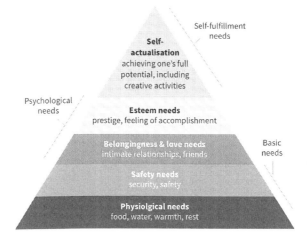

Most often portrayed in the shape of a five-tiered pyramid, Maslow's Hierarchy of Needs demonstrates that once basic needs are fulfilled, the individual moves up the pyramid to the next stage—from physiological, safety, love, and esteem needs to the need for self-fulfillment.

Maslow's basic premise is, "What man can be, he must be." He asserts that humans at the top of their game need to experience purpose and meaning in their lives. The highest degree of intellectual achievement, according to Maslow, is self-actualization.

Late in his life, he criticized his own work, recognizing that realizing one's potential was only half of self-actualization. The other "you complete me" half was transcendence—helping others realize *their* potential.

Combining Maslow's original hierarchy with his later inclusion of transcendence provides a remixed and remastered version we're calling your personal legend—fulfilling your life's spiritual purpose.

The life you live is the outward expression of your inner journey.

∽✕∾

Personal legends support and reinforce all of our needs: physical, mental, emotional, and spiritual. They awaken us to answer the call, take the leap, and pursue our destiny. A personal legend is a spiritual call challenging us to answer the questions: *Why am I here? Am I serving a purpose greater than myself?*

A personal legend is not a collection of stories about how great your life has been. It's not about how well you perform or how successful you are in your career. Your legend is not what you've accomplished for yourself or what is chiseled on your tombstone.

A personal legend informs and directs the overarching purpose of our life. Like the legend on a map that explains the symbols and what they mean, the personal legend guides us along the Map of Self-Discovery.

The subconscious mind uses symbols to sort and code information. The personal legend speaks the language of the mind influencing our decisions while providing direction on the path of our dreams. Understanding our legend and manifesting our purpose is what brings us joy and enthusiasm.

In *The Alchemist*, Paulo Coelho tells the story of the shepherd boy Santiago sleeping under a sycamore tree. In his recurring dream, he is told, "If you come here, you will find a hidden treasure." Santiago sets out on a quest to discover his treasure—a journey to realize his personal legend.

Santiago makes the most important choice of his life: pursuing his personal legend. Along his path, he meets his mentor, gains many allies, fends off troublesome enemies, and experiences love.

184

Near the end of the story, Santiago realizes that finding his treasure wasn't nearly as rewarding as the journey itself. He learned much, lived purposefully, and loved well—none of which would have happened had he been told exactly where to find his hidden treasure buried right under the sycamore tree where the story begins.

We grasp our legend when we undergo transformation. Napping under a tree takes us nowhere. Similar to alchemy, where lead is transformed into gold, we transform our full potential into the best version of ourselves: self-actualization.

Everyone has a personal legend, but not everyone chooses to pursue it. Santiago wasn't looking for his personal legend; he set out on a journey to *realize* it.

Author Paulo Coelho said, "You know that you have a reason to be here. It's the only thing that gives you enthusiasm." *The Alchemist* was certainly his personal legend; Coelho passionately wrote the book in only two weeks. He explained the story was "already written in my soul."

As you weave new storylines into your personal action-adventure and write new chapters into your life you never imagined possible, consider the cumulative as well as incremental effects of pursuing your personal legend—a process more valuable than gold.

> "What you still need to know is this: before a dream is realized, the Soul of the World tests everything that was learned along the way. It does this not because it is evil, but so that we can, in addition to realizing our dreams, master the lessons we've learned as we've moved toward that dream."
> ~ *The Alchemist*

185

LIVING IN ESSENCE

Essence is the intrinsic nature and essential qualities of an individual. It is an extract or concentrate from the very center of your being. Essence is hard to capture because it is full of fleeting mystical moments—although it is sometimes possible to capture the essence of someone in a good photograph.

Essence is *not* your personality. Persona is your mask, the identity that facilitates hiding the real you—your essence. Persona is a direct report to the ego, which commands every calculated move of the personality. Essence is independent of the ego. In our essence, we are here to serve others, whereas the ego is all about serving itself.

The inner journey is one from identity to essence. Michael Hauge sees the transformation as "the necessary death of one's identity in order to be fulfilled and achieve one's destiny." When you strip away the mask and everything you're attached to (home, car, job, looks, money), what's left? This is your essence. This is who you really are.

Essence is not your story. It may be an excellent contributor to your story, but it is not the story itself. We tell our stories so often and so convincingly that we end up believing them even when they're not in our best interest. Our stories can hijack our lives to the point that we're living day to day to fulfill our self-proclaimed sad existence.

We get married to our stories not because we believe they support our best efforts and challenge us beyond our comfort zone. We attach ourselves to limiting beliefs because they're comfortable and require little effort. Don't let your story commandeer your quest.

So, if essence isn't your personality or your story, what is it?

Essence is like your *style*—how you express your inner being. Like the invisible gift of intuition, essence is more of an intangible, ethereal presence.

Essence might best be described in the alchemy of perfume. Forego the individual components of fragrant essential oils or

186

aromatic compounds. It is not the chemicals but the chemistry that surrounds us when we combine it with our body's heat, oils, and aromas. It is unique to us and permeates our being. It is everywhere, and it is nowhere. What would you be doing if you were living in your essence? Here are some possibilities:

- Living from the heart
- Sharing your gifts and talents
- Lighting the fires of your passion
- Harmonizing with the world around you
- Understanding why you are here
- Expressing yourself creatively
- Living life on purpose

Aristotle believed the energy of the mind is the essence of life. When you know what you love, what you're good at, what you're passionate about, and what your purpose is, you're feeding your essence. In turn, your essence nourishes your spirit.

I enjoy crafting a good sentence (weird, I know). Better yet, I love composing a complete paragraph that sings. I express my inner being through the creative endeavors of writing and photography. My essence is composed of learning, sharing, teaching, and collaborating. It's all those things and none of them at any given moment. When mixed with my passion, purpose, gifts, and talents, the resulting chemistry becomes my essence.

Living in my essence enables me to help people discover their life path by charting new adventures in personal growth and lifelong learning. I gain fulfillment in my life purpose and serve others at the same time.

Essence is everything you are and everything you are meant to be. Within the seeds of knowledge and understanding, you find inspiration and motivation. The cycle becomes self-perpetuating. The experience and wisdom acquired on life's path enable you to live from the inside out.

Living in your essence provides a well-nourished co-creator for realizing your best self—your personal legend.

BECOMING THE MASTER

At the beginning of this book, we asked the crucial questions: *What is the meaning of life? Who am I? What on earth am I doing here?*

The absence of meaning and purpose leaves us numb and directionless. Heroes on a quest find any way possible to return with at least some semblance of meaning. Each of us reconciles these questions and finds the answers within ourselves while living the Hero's Journey.

Gregg Levoy believes life doesn't end with answers, but with another question: *What next?* A new beginning begs your attention and participation. The story requires an action hero in the role of a lifetime.

The circle of learning, the circle of life, takes us around the continuous loop of awareness/change/renewal. Each new level enlightens us to a better version of ourselves—one that was inside just waiting to burst out and flourish.

Where are you on your journey? Where are you in the evolutionary order? Are you just getting by, or have you evolved up the hierarchy? Have you arrived at a level that enables you to give back and pay it forward?

The ego helps you survive and thrive. The soul helps you serve and support. Is it your turn to step up and shift roles? Is it time to open your eyes to your destiny, to your real purpose in life? If not, that's okay. Only you know if you're fooling yourself and stunting your fullest potential.

The role of the hero is to serve and to sacrifice. The role of the master is to enlighten and to embolden. As the mentor, you freely share your wisdom and inspire confidence.

If you're at the point now where you're thinking, "Yeah, service, I'll get to that later," just know that is a refusal of the call. You are here for a reason. You have been created for a purpose, and if you choose, you may pursue your legend and fulfill your destiny. It's always been your choice.

The meaning of life is mysteriously revealed in the act of giving. According to Matthew Kelly, author of *The Rhythm of Life*, there is no faster way to discover the purpose of your life than to "embrace the daily opportunities to serve those around you."

"You have been born to live one life," Kelly states. "Nobody else has been entrusted with your role in human history. If you do not play your part, your part will go unplayed." Think about it. What would it be like if you opted out? How would the world be different had you never been born?

It's difficult not to think about Jimmy Stewart playing the role of George Bailey in the 1946 film *It's a Wonderful Life*. George wishes he had never been born and gets to see what the world would look like without him.

In this alternate reality, George's beloved community of Bedford Falls is instead named Pottersville, after the greedy banker. Many of George's friends and relatives that he helped along the way are now down and out, in prison, or worse. His brother Harry died as a child when George wasn't there to save him from drowning after breaking through the ice and falling into freezing water. Harry never goes on to become a war hero, and all the soldiers he would have saved also die. George's guardian spirit, Clarence, tells him, "Strange, isn't it? Each man's life touches so many other lives, and when he isn't around, he leaves an awful hole, doesn't he?"

The choice is yours. You can embrace your role and bring meaning to yourself and to the world, or you can opt out. No one will be the wiser. It will be like you were never born.

Mythologist Joseph Campbell believed that life is inherently without meaning and that you bring meaning to it. If you follow your bliss, he says, "You put yourself on a kind of track that has been there all the while waiting for you, and the life you ought to be living is the one you are living."

BORN TO FLOURISH

Contrary to how the world is presented to you on a daily basis, regardless of the number of obstacles placed in front of you, no matter what challenges you face each day, know this: You were born to flourish.

Understandably, there are times you may not feel like you were born to flourish, but you were. If you are flourishing, you are following your path. If you don't feel like you're already flourishing, you will. It can't be helped. It is your destiny. Unless, of course, you won't allow it. It's strictly up to you. It's your choice and yours alone.

"You were born to win," says motivational speaker Zig Ziglar, but to be a winner, you must plan to win, prepare to win, and expect to win. The paradox, is you must be willing to fail first. Avoid failure, and you also avoid success. They are two sides of the same coin. Failure is the path to success. Without the willingness to walk through your fear of failure, you will never succeed in reaching your destiny.

Don't worry, failing is easy. You may have already done it a time or two. Going forward, relax in the knowledge that failure is the key to learning.

Many people don't know how to learn. To a large degree, school smarts are based on memorization. In traditional education, lessons come first—then no mistakes are permitted. With "street smarts," mistakes come first, and then it's up to you to learn the lesson. Both forms of education are expensive, albeit in different ways.

Personal growth is a solo sport. The only person you're competing against is yourself. Self-help books can be motivational, but recognize their limitations—they're not about you. They're about the individual who wrote them and about the people with whom the author relates (this book included). Make the story about you and customize your personal growth.

Tap into the wealth of knowledge you've already accumulated, and the right choices emerge. Whether you realize it or not, you already know the next move you need to make, the next goal to pursue, the next dragon you need to slay. What most of us don't know is how to uncover that hidden knowledge and act upon it. My sincere hope is that *Living the Hero's Journey* has given you the inspiration to take action on your dreams.

As we unwind in the final stage of the Hero's Journey, let me say what a pleasure it has been to be part of your action-adventure. What a long, hard road it's been—but isn't that where all the living happens?

What has living the Hero's Journey come to mean for you? What does "living" really mean? Is it different from what you thought when you began this book? I know it is different for me now from what it was when I started writing this book. Isn't it interesting how we look at life differently the further we get into it—especially when there's more of life behind us than in front of us?

In any great story or intriguing screenplay, there is irony. Dramatic irony provides the reader or moviegoer with an item of information of which the hero in the narrative is unaware. At the end of *Raiders of the Lost Ark*, for example, Indy is assured that "top men" are studying the Ark. The final shot of the movie focuses on the wooden crate in which the Ark is sealed. The camera pulls back slowly to reveal it surrounded by countless other similar crates. Pulling back even further, we see an enormous, dimly lit, never-ending government warehouse full of sealed wooden crates.

The irony here is that while we feel compelled to define our path in life, there is no destination in reaching our destiny. As Santiago learned, life well lived is about the journey—a Hero's Journey that makes all the difference in the world.

I trust you are well on your way.

EXPLORING YOUR ROLE

We have come full circle. The circle of learning takes us around the continuous loop of awareness/change/renewal. Another journey around the monomyth is the circle of life.

Know thyself, and you will know you were born to flourish. Knowing yourself well + being passionate about your purpose + living in your essence = a high quality of life.

- You own the life you deserve. Think you deserve more? Then *be* more.
- The life you live is the outward expression of your inner journey.
- Life is inherently meaningless. The meaning life receives is what you bring to it.

It is a basic human need to experience purpose and meaning. Each of us reconciles the meaning of our lives while living the Hero's Journey.

The inner journey is one from our ego identity to our core essence. In essence, we are here to serve others.

The path to fulfilling our life's spiritual purpose is found in our personal legend. The legend guides us along the Map of Self-Discovery.

The meaning of life is mysteriously revealed in the act of giving. We must acquiesce to our excellence so we may deliver the gift we were brought into this world to convey.

Barely a gleam in the twinkle of an unconscious eye, your great-great-grandkids, whom you will never meet, have an opportunity to live a better life—because you dared to be the hero of *your* life.

ᴓ Self-Discovery ᴓ

1. Who is responsible for the life you're now living? Who has the power to change what's not working?
2. Is there a story you tell yourself and others that is hijacking your life—limiting your potential?
3. What would you be doing differently if you were living in your essence?
4. Is it your turn to give back and pay it forward—to step up and shift roles to serve and support?

CHAPTER 14

LIVES WELL LIVED

Happiness is not a goal . . . it's a
by product of a life well lived.
~ Eleanor Roosevelt

L iving well. This is the long-term goal I wrote down after listening to an Earl Nightingale audio cassette decades ago in Orlando, Florida. The definition of "living well" has changed for me significantly since then. The overall sentiment persists.

When I sold my training company years ago, it looked like I had finally arrived. I was ready to step into the good life. Now I could be happy and content. And why not? I had earned my success and paid my dues (for nearly a lifetime).

Based on what I now recognize as social conditioning, I thought the appropriate thing to do would be to find paradise, move there, and kick back with my family. This began a five-year expedition around the world to discover Shangri-La (and shoot a few photos).

When I first began chasing paradise, my expectations were something akin to what was seen in the television show *Fantasy Island* (1977–84). Island overseer Mr. Rourke (Ricardo Montalbán) begins each episode in his tailored white suit, reminding the resort's attentive staff, "Smiles. Smiles, everyone. We want our guests to feel welcome."

The show's premise is simple yet powerful: Entertain affluent guests on a remote tropical island in luxurious surroundings, and make their secret dreams come true. I don't know too many people who wouldn't sign on for that experience. It still tugs at me.

When I learned to let go of the fictional fantasy of paradise, a seed of truth began to sprout. It took years for it to come into full bloom, but I now know what I'm looking for and where to find it (better late than never).

Paradise isn't just a place. It's a purpose. It's a passion. Living in paradise constitutes a total "you-friendly" environment in which you can fully immerse yourself in the elixir of life: grace, goodness, and gratitude. The quest for paradise turns out to be an unnecessarily long journey—especially considering where you'll find it—but don't let that stop you from planting seeds along the way.

Smiles, everyone.

FLOURISHING IN FULFILLMENT

Living well is on everyone's wish list, but each of us enjoys a slightly different flavor of flourishing. The more revolutions we take around the Map of Self-Discovery, the wiser we become. We become more attuned to what is meaningful and important versus what is frivolous and temporary.

As you might imagine, the ancient philosophers had some experience in this arena. Let's look to our model mentor, Aristotle, for some insights. In 350 BC he wrote an essay titled "Nichomachean Ethics." If you think that's hard to say, just wait till you try to pronounce the topic: *eudaimonia.*

Depending on who's translating the word (it's all Greek to me), *eudaimonia* means "well-being, happiness, fulfillment, and/or human flourishing." Etymologically, the word is a mashup of *eu* (good) and *daimōn* (spirit). For Aristotle, it was the proper goal of a life well lived: practicing the virtues in one's everyday life.

Fellow Greek philosopher Epicurus agreed with Aristotle that eudaimonia is the highest good, but put a different spin on it. The Epicurean school of philosophy was less about high moral values and more about the modest pleasures of happiness, tranquility, and freedom.

Some consider flourishing to mean taking it easy and enjoying the good life with all the amusements and distractions that go with it. Others see themselves flourishing with the acquisition and accumulation of wealth and power. Still others regard it as the pursuit of honor and a life dedicated to public service.

I'm in favor of the literal translation of "good spirit." Like the guardian spirit—our personal guide in the previous chapter— there's something inspiring about co-creating the decisions leading to our best life. Should that be a life of honor, a life of pleasure, or a life of virtue?

As in nature, flourishing requires balance. Too much of one component and not enough of the other weakens the spirit. The balance prescribed for moving forward is living well and doing well—living the good life while contributing the highest value for the greatest good.

"Flourishing goes beyond happiness, or satisfaction with life," says University of North Carolina psychology professor Barbara Fredrickson. "True, people who flourish are happy. But that's not the half of it. Beyond feeling good, they're also doing good—adding value to the world."

The concepts of happiness, flourishing, and highest good sound a lot like self-actualization, don't they? Not only is it easier to say than eudaimonia, but self-actualization is more familiar to us—with good reason.

In the early 1960s, there was a faction in the psychology community that viewed Sigmund Freud's theories of psychoanalysis as limiting and overly pessimistic. Psychologists Carl Rogers and Abraham Maslow started remixing the best of eudaimonia hits from the era of Socrates through the time of the Renaissance. The resulting study of human behavior with emphasis on the whole person became a smash hit: Humanistic Psychology.

Maslow and Rogers pioneered a kinder, gentler "person-centered" therapy with the foundational belief that people are inherently good—a forerunner to today's Positive Psychology movement. The two trailblazers believed, "[Self-actualization] can be achieved when all basic and mental needs are essentially fulfilled and the 'actualization' of the full personal potential takes place." Usable translation: Self-actualization is recognizing and expressing your gifts and talents with a creative flair.

HAPPINESS OF PURSUIT

Pursuing happiness is a lifelong obsession for most of us. I know it was for me. Even though I desire happiness just as much as the next guy, I've learned that real happiness comes in the pursuit of the challenge, not as the "just reward."

With all due respect to Thomas Jefferson, who thought it important enough to include in the Declaration of Independence, the direct pursuit of happiness is a fool's errand. It may be an "inalienable right," but it's not going to get us where we long to be. Much like chasing the pot of gold at the end of the rainbow, we're never going to seize happiness.

Joy and happiness are not emotions that can be chased with any degree of success—they must be authentically earned. Happiness is a difficult job well done; it includes overcoming unforeseen obstacles and beating the odds. Our most rewarding and fulfilling times come after struggle. We know this subconsciously, but there's an instinct in human beings that takes the perceived shortest route requiring the least amount of effort for any given task. For some, pursuing happiness sounds a lot better than earning it, so they follow their instinct (or wishful thinking). Why this path of pursuit is followed is no mystery; it's human nature.

Happiness is most heartfelt when we're there for someone. They feel better, we feel better. These feelings can be multiplied exponentially, according to two professors at the University of California, Berkeley: "Happiness is found in actions that lift up the welfare in as many people as possible." Dacher Keltner and Emiliana Simon-Thomas teach The Science of Happiness, arguably the most popular course on campus. They say, "Happiness may not be about your own personal pleasure or the delights you experience, but rather it's about bringing a lot of good to other people. It's about lifting up communities as a way to define happiness."

Isn't this what larger-than-life action heroes do in the movies? In one way or another, they "save the world." The question becomes: What can we do to save our corner of the world? Are we willing to make the sacrifices necessary to live up to our potential and fulfill our purpose in being here?

Admittedly, I missed the boat on this one. I thought I had brought good to people and lifted the community. Over the span of ten years, I had built a coach training organization that taught thousands of individuals to be life coaches, who then went on to coach tens of thousands of clients toward a better life. I flourished during this time and enjoyed a tremendous amount of gratification.

When I sold the business, it was the culmination of a major life goal. I had helped a lot of people and done well for myself at the same time. I couldn't be happier. Then—poof!—it was gone. Hey, what happened to all the happiness I had pursued so diligently? This is where I was supposed to collect, right?

The pursuit of happiness left me at a dead end. There wasn't anything there. All this time I had been waiting to arrive, to be happy, and to live well. Now that I was here, all I could think was, *What was all this talk about goals and success?*

Carl Rogers observed, "The good life is a process, not a state of being." Arriving at our destination and achieving our goal is like eating great Chinese food—wonderful in the moment, but an hour later, we're hungry again. We need the next challenge, the next goal, the next struggle. Instinctively, we know that's where the juice is. Happiness comes as the organic byproduct of the journey itself.

A life well lived is not about the hero reaching her destination. It's about the quality of life while living the Hero's Journey. Our goal may be to watch a feel-good movie. When the movie is over, we've accomplished our goal. Does this make us happy, or were we happiest when we were experiencing the sights, sounds, and emotions within the film?

Goals are overrated. Enjoy the good life while it's happening. Yes, it's valuable to know where you're headed and why you want to get there. Just don't forget to breathe in the joy and happiness along the way. When you look back, these pleasing memories will be filed under A Life Well Lived.

Let your work be your reward. Better yet, let your life's work be your legacy.

In real estate, a perfectly good house or building will be torn down and replaced with something better suited for that property. It's called "highest and best use" of the land. What's your highest and best use? What needs to be razed so you can deliver your highest value? How do you need to reinvent yourself and repackage your gift? The level of your success comes in direct proportion to the number of people you help.

Actor Robert De Niro, in an interview about his role in the film *Everybody's Fine*, summed it up this way, "You need a sense of purpose. You find something you really love and then you follow through. You stick with it. Nothing is easy if you really want to do it well or feel good about yourself. You've got to work at it. And in that work, well . . . there's your happiness."

FROM SUCCESS TO SIGNIFICANCE

Personal success has many forms and can mean different things to different people. It usually involves career, finances, and social standing. Success is a measure of control one has over the outside world that then quantifies a person's inner value. The flow of energy and value comes from outside the individual and is internalized.

Significance flows from the inside out. Significance is what we give back, pay forward, and bestow upon others. It is the gift of experience and wisdom that radiates out from people who know what to do with their achievement. It's easy to become consumed with navigating our way to success. When we finally arrive, however, we discover that the landing zone is actually a launch pad.

Success is the launch pad to significance.

Are you living for leisure or leaving a legacy? Are you keeping your feet on the ground and being practical, or are you launching yourself from success to significance? What will you do with your success and the treasures you've brought back from your journey?

Success can leave one in a precarious state. Once you achieve a major goal, you lose your purpose. The void left by purpose and passion easily fills with aimlessness and depression.

When I achieved success, I kicked back and watched my gift—the elixir I was to share with the world—just sitting on the shelf not helping anyone, least of all me. How am I bouncing back from the pitfalls of success (only half-joking)? I am repurposing myself and re-sparking my essence. This book is my humble launch pad on a quest toward significance. Will I make it? I'd like to think so, but even if it doesn't work out the way I hope, I'm soaking it all in this time and enjoying the journey.

Joseph Campbell wrote "The whole idea is that you've got to bring out again that which you went to recover, the unrealized, unutilized potential in yourself," (Campbell, 2004). Heroes do the hard things and ask the tough questions. My colleague at Coach Training Alliance, David Krueger, asks himself each night, "What have I done today that will live beyond tomorrow?" Pondering the answer is a great thing to sleep on. Are you making a difference? Are you contributing something of substance and significance? Living up to your potential is hard work and something best achieved with the help of others—namely, coaches and mentors.

Most of us spend so much of our lives chasing success that we don't even recognize it when we've finally caught up with it. We just keep running after more, bigger, and better. Persistence, which served us well as a virtue, now becomes a vice. We continue doing more of the same because it's the norm. Pulitzer Prize–winning journalist Ellen Goodman recognized, "Normal is getting dressed in clothes that you buy for work and driving through traffic in a car that you are still paying for . . . in order to get to the job you need to pay for the clothes and the car, and the house you leave vacant all day so you can afford to live in it."

How many successful people do you know who still live the rat race even though they're in a better position than most to lead a life of significance? Maybe that someone is close to you—real close, like the person who squints at you every morning in the mirror.

We complete this revolution of the Hero's Journey by returning to the place where we began—the known, ordinary world. We feel a bit exhausted, but a lot stronger and much wiser. Our transformation positions us for living our lives to match our potential. What an honor and responsibility this is.

This book coming to an end marks, for you, a fresh beginning. It's been a privilege accompanying you on this stretch of the path, and I trust you'll find the Map of Self-Discovery helpful on future quests.

If you look down at your feet, there is an untrodden path revealing itself before you. A new expedition is emerging from your awareness that is wrapped in more action and adventure than you can possibly imagine.

I'll leave you with three aphorisms to take with you as you continue living the Hero's Journey:

1. Life isn't easy. Don't expect it to be.

2. You were born to flourish. Live well.

3. You are the hero of your life. Act like it.

NEXT STEPS

"Much to learn, you still have."

~ Master Yoda

I't's time to put thought into action. For many, good intentions are as far as they get. For you, let's make it real and actionable. We begin with gifts from the mentor.

YOUR WISH IS MY COMMAND

Expanding the Power of Your Personal Genie

The genie we all have inside us is awaiting our instructions and ready to grant our every wish.

If you're not where you want to be in life, what commands are you giving your genie? Listen to this enchanting tale embroiling your greatest ally and your worst enemy.

Just rub the magic lamp at: **willcraig.com/gifts**

DISCOVERING PURPOSE & PASSION

Assessment and Guidance

Like two sides of the same coin, purpose and passion are inseparable. These two life forces are entwined in a captivating, fiery dance with destiny. No wonder we find them so alluring.

If you've ever found yourself saying, "I'd be happy to follow my passion, if I only knew what it was," this assessment is for you.

Ignite the flame within you at: **willcraig.com/gifts**

205

UNCOVER YOUR LIFE PATH

Ever wish you had a map to guide you on your life path? You're in luck! Activate this enchanted, visionary blueprint for personal growth—**with your name on it**—at willcraig.com.

Unroll the Map of Self-Discovery as my gift. You'll be needing this on your inner journey. The map discloses the symbols, metaphors, and rites of passage that provide direction and expose the ideal path right beneath your feet.

Activate your map at: **willcraig.com**

THE MENTOR SESSIONS
Living the Hero's Journey Guidebook

Meeting your mentor is one of the most exciting stages of the journey. You'll be introduced to eight different mentors each imparting life lessons and life-shaping knowledge. This companion guidebook takes you deeper into understanding yourself and revealing your true purpose.

The guidebook includes:
- Personal assessments and worksheets
- Weekly audio mentoring sessions
- Evolving challenge assignments
- Map of Self-Discovery–full interactive version

The mysterious inner workings of the Hero's Journey are uncovered and become an indispensable travel guide for you to follow on your journey of a lifetime.

Go to: **willcraig.com/nextstep**

207

ABOUT THE AUTHOR

Will Craig is a writer and photographer who travels the world researching and documenting the subtleties and nuances of a life well lived. As an avid explorer, the odyssey that fascinates him the most is the inner journey. Will's passion is creating dynamic stories using engaging content and captured moments.

Will shares the paths traveled, lessons learned, and insights gained over the course of a decade as the founder and former dean of an international coaching and mentoring company based in Boulder, Colorado. He holds a master's degree in Education and Human Development from The George Washington University in Washington, D.C.

Will Craig has worked with entertainment giants like the Walt Disney Company, Up with People, and Universal Studios. For twelve years, he was a writer-producer of film and television projects and served as president of the Florida Motion Picture & Television Association.

Pay It Forward

It has been an honor to walk this part of life's path with you. Please share your experience of *Living the Hero's Journey*. Let others know what you think and what to expect by leaving an honest review at: Amzn.to/2uoHhSc. Thank you.

BIBLIOGRAPHY
Further Reading and Resources

BOOKS

Beckwith, M.B. (2010) *Spiritual liberation: Fulfilling your soul's potential.* Philadelphia, PA, United States: Simon & Schuster Adult Publishing Group.

Brown, B.C. (2010) *The gifts of imperfection: Let go of who you think you're supposed to be and embrace who you are.* Philadelphia, PA, United States: Hazelden Information & Educational Services.

Brown, D. (2009) *The da Vinci code: A novel.* 2nd edn. New York: Knopf Doubleday Publishing Group.

Burchard, B. (2014) *The motivation manifesto: 9 declarations to claim your personal power.* United States: Hay House.

Campbell, J. (1972) *Myths to live by.* New York: Viking Press.

Campbell, J. (1991) *Reflections on the art of living,* Joseph Campbell Foundation.

Campbell, J. (1992) *The masks of god: V. 4: Creative mythology.* New York: Penguin Group (USA).

Campbell, J. (2003) *The hero's journey: Joseph Campbell on his life and work.* Edited by Phil Cousineau. United States: Publishers Group West.

Campbell, J. (2004) *Pathways to bliss.* Joseph Campbell Foundation.

Campbell, J. (2008) *The hero with a thousand faces.* Novato: New World Library.

Campbell, J. and Moyers, B.D. (1988) *The power of myth.* New York, NY: Doubleday Books.

Canfield, J. and Switzer, J. (2006) *The success principles: How to get from where you are to where you want to be.* New York: HarperCollins Publishers.

Coelho, P. (2014) *The alchemist.* New York, NY, United States: HarperCollins Publishers.

Cousineau, P. (2001) *Once and future myths: The power of ancient stories in modern times.* Berkeley, CA: Conari Press, U.S.

211

Dyer, W.W. (2007) *Change your thoughts - change your life: Living the wisdom of the Tao*. Carlsbad, CA: Hay House.

Fielding, H. and Aristotle (1957) *Aristotle's poetics*. Cambridge, MA, United States: Harvard University Press.

Ford, D. and Boberg-Shalyi, S. (2008) *The secret of the shadow: The power of owning your story*. United States: HarperCollins.

Gelb, M.J. (2000) *How to think like Leonardo da Vinci: Seven steps to genius every day*. New York, NY: Bantam Doubleday Dell Publishing Group.

Keen, S. and Valley-Fox, A. (1989) *Your mythic journey: Finding meaning in your life through writing and storytelling*. Los Angeles: Penguin Group (USA).

Kelly, M. (2006) *The rhythm of life: Living every day with passion and purpose*. New York: Simon & Schuster Adult Publishing Group.

Levoy, G. (1998) *Callings: Finding and following an authentic life*. New York: Crown Publishing Group.

Marsh, N. (2007) *Fat, forty and fired*. Sydney: Bantam.

Maslow, A.H. (1970) *Motivation and personality*. 3rd edn. New York: Addison-Wesley Educational Publishers.

May, M.E. (2009) *In pursuit of elegance: Why the best ideas have something missing*. New York: Crown Publishing Group.

Meade, M. (2010) *Fate and destiny: The two agreements of the soul*. Seattle, WA: Greenfire Press.

Myss, C. (2003) *Sacred contracts: Awakening your divine potential*. New York: Crown Publishing Group.

O'Donohue, J. (2008) *Anam Cara: A book of Celtic wisdom*. New York, NY, United States: HarperCollins Publishers.

Ohotto, R. (2009) *Transforming fate into destiny: A new dialogue with your soul*. Carlsbad, CA: Hay House.

Ruiz, D.M. (1997) *The four agreements: A practical guide to personal freedom*. San Rafael, CA: Publishers Group West.

Sebold, A. (2004) *The lovely bones: A novel*. New York: Little, Brown & Company.

Tolle, E. (2008) *A new earth: Awakening to your life's purpose*. London: Penguin Group (USA).

Turner, M. (1998) *The literary mind*. New York: Oxford University Press, USA.

Vogler, C. (2007) *The writer's journey: Mythic structure for writers*. 3rd edn. United States: Wiese, Michael Productions.

Ziglar, Z. (1975) *See you at the top*. New York, NY, United States: Pelican Publishing Co.

FILMS

It's a wonderful life (1946) Directed by Frank Capra RKO Radio Pictures.
Moana (2016) Directed by Ron Clements, Don Hall Walt Disney Studios.

Aladdin (1992) Directed by Ron Clements, John Musker Walt Disney Studios.

Harry Potter and the sorcerer's stone (2001) Directed by Chris Columbus Warner Bros.

The godfather (1972) Directed by Francis Ford Coppola Paramount Pictures.

Snow white and the Seven dwarfs (1937) Directed by William Cottrell Walt Disney Studios.

The wizard of oz (1939) Directed by Victor Fleming Metro Goldwyn Mayer.

Sleeping beauty (1959) Directed by Clyde Geronimi Walt Disney Studios.
Braveheart (1995) Directed by Mel Gibson 20th Century Fox.

An officer and a gentleman (1982) Directed by Taylor Hackford Paramount Pictures.

Butch Cassidy and the Sundance kid (1969) Directed by George Roy Hill 20th Century Fox.
The da Vinci code (2006) Directed by Ron Howard Sony / Columbia.
Sliding doors (1998) Directed by Peter Howitt Paramount Pictures.

The lord of the rings: The fellowship of the ring (2001) Directed by Peter Jackson New Line Cinema.

The Hobbit: An unexpected journey (2012) Directed by Peter Jackson New Line Cinema.
Cars (2006) Directed by John Lasseter, Joe Ranft Walt Disney Studios.

Fantasy Island (1977) Directed by Gene Levitt Sony Pictures Television.

Mr. & Mrs. Smith (2005) Directed by Doug Liman 20th Century Fox.

Star Wars: Episode IV - A new hope (1977) Directed by George Lucas 20th Century Fox.

Groundhog day (1993) Directed by Harold Ramis Columbia Pictures.

Raiders of the lost Ark (1981) Directed by Steven Spielberg Paramount Pictures.

Indiana Jones and the last crusade (1989) Directed by Steven Spielberg Paramount Pictures.

Saving private Ryan (1998) Directed by Steven Spielberg DreamWorks.

The power of myth (1988) [DVD]. New York: The Independent Production Fund.

Beauty and the beast (1991) Directed by Gary Trousdale, Kirk Wise Walt Disney Studios.

Good will hunting (1997) Directed by Gus Van Sant Miramax.

The matrix (1999) Directed by Lana Wachowski Warner Bros.

Dead poets society (1989) Directed by Peter Weir Touchstone Pictures.

Romancing the stone (1984) Directed by Robert Zemeckis 20th Century Fox.

WEBSITES

Belsten, Ph.D, Laura. (2016) *CEO Partnership*. Available at: http://CEOPartnership.com.

Black, Ph.D., Jackie. (1999) *Dr. Jackie Black*. Available at: http://drjackieblack.com.

Brown-Volkman, D. (2016) *Surpass Your Dreams*. Available at: http://surpassyourdreams.com.

Glaser, Judith E. (2017) *Creating WE: A benchmark communications standard of excellence*. Available at: http://www.creatingwe.com.

Hauge, Michael. (2014) *Story mastery*. Available at: http://www.storymastery.com.

Herdlinger, David. (2016) *Kashbox coaching.* Available at:
http://www.herdlinger.com.

Hess, Rhonda. (2007) *Prosperous Coach.* Available at:
http://prosperouscoachblog.com.

JCF (2016) *Joseph Campbell Foundation.* Available at:
http://www.jcf-myth.org.

Krueger, MD, David. (2016) *Mentor Mindsets.* Available at:
http://www.mentorpath.com.

Leshinsky, Milana. (2016) *Simplicity Circle.* Available at:
http://milana.com/blog.

Redford, Robert. (2016) *Sundance institute.* Available at:
http://www.sundance.org.

Sirois, Maria. (2016) *Maria Sirois, Psy.D.* Available at:
http://mariasirois.com.

UC-Berkeley (2016) *The science of happiness.* Available at:
http://greatergood.berkeley.edu/news_events/event/the_science_
of_happiness.

Vogler, Christopher. (2016) *The writer's journey.* Available at:
http://www.thewritersjourney.com.

Made in the USA
Middletown, DE
16 July 2019